T0198528

Spirituality and Scientific Strategies for Managing Your Emotions

Using Your Emotional Intelligence Skills, EQ

What stories do you tell yourself about how you manage your emotions?
Why are you where you are in your life's journey?

Pollis Robertson, PhD

WESTBOW
P R E S S®
A DIVISION OF THOMAS NELSON
& ZONDERVAN

WestBow Press books may be ordered through booksellers or by contacting:

WestBow Press
A Division of Thomas Nelson & Zondervan
1663 Liberty Drive
Bloomington, IN 47403
www.westbowpress.com
1 (866) 928-1240

Unless otherwise noted, scripture quotations are taken from the Holy Bible, New Living Translation, Copyright © 1996, 2004, 2015 by Tyndale House Foundation. Used by permission of Tyndale House Publishers, Inc., Carol Stream, Illinois 60188. All rights reserved.

Scripture quotations marked KJV are taken from the King James Version of the Bible.

Scripture quotations marked (NIV) are taken from the Holy Bible, New International Version®, NIV®. Copyright © 1973, 1978, 1984, 2011 by Biblica, Inc.™ Used by permission of Zondervan. All rights reserved worldwide. www.zondervan.comThe "NIV" and "New International Version" are trademarks registered in the United States Patent and Trademark Office by Biblica, Inc.™

ISBN: 978-1-9736-6845-9 (sc)
ISBN: 978-1-9736-6846-6 (hc)
ISBN: 978-1-9736-6844-2 (e)

Library of Congress Control Number: 2019908959

Print information available on the last page.

WestBow Press rev. date: 01/27/2020

Contents

Part IV   Emotional Management and Greater Decision-Making Efficacy

Part V   Appendices

Preface

This book is about understanding and managing one's emotions. It serves as a practical guide for those who are concerned about improving their emotional intelligence. My original goal in writing this book was to give readers a short, fun read with both scientific and spiritual principles that have stood the test of time.

> You will discover that this book provides many valuable research findings, quotes, and insights that are helpful in developing effective emotional management strategies. The readers will easily identify these strategies in the book by the boxed text areas.

However, my passion for writing this book stems from my background as a child of lower working-class parents with little formal education. After years of observing, studying, and practicing human behavioral scientific principles in my professional occupation, I discovered that most studies on emotional control have largely focused on the middle to upper end of the social classes. The contrast between what is found in these studies and what I have experienced as an African American from a lower working-class family inspired me to more fully explore the vastly different perspectives of the upper and middle classes when compared to the working poor and lower-class families.

One purpose of this book is to help readers discover why individuals from various social classes, as defined by Dennis Gilbert (1996), often respond differently to situations that require emotional control. This book also highlights the difference between simply controlling one's emotions and effectively managing one's emotions. It demonstrates that the latter is an absolute must for an enriched personal life and a successful professional career in today's relationship-driven society.

In combining my passion with my purpose, my goal is to make this book more reflective of the important issues facing society and give readers a book that will inspire them to want to learn more about emotional management and personal and professional relationship management. Therefore, the structure of this book for each chapter consists of three main areas. First, each chapter begins with a story from my life and a parable from the Bible that relates to the story. The life stories reflect actual incidents or situations that affected my life and influenced my behavior. I have changed the names of individuals and places to protect the privacy of the individuals. I present the middle-socioeconomic to the lower-socioeconomic classes' views to help readers better understand how their views would differ from someone in the upper-socioeconomic classes. Second, I present important scientific principles on emotional control and the important spiritual principles on emotional control. I discuss the importance of using both science and spirituality to resolve the issues presented in the chapters' stories.

Finally, I discuss the important lessons readers can learn from each chapter's story. I discuss how the scientific and spiritual principles when used appropriately in society will enhance personal well-being from the individuals' perspectives of social, emotional, spiritual, and physical well-being. In addition, I emphasize the importance of the environmental perspective of interpersonal, local, national, and global relationship management skills development.

I use many of the recent findings of interpersonal neurobiology as it relates to emotional and social intelligence as one of the scientific models for much of the information in this book. I used the Bible as the spiritual model to demonstrate how Christian principles as taught in many Christian churches help individuals manage their emotions even more effectively.

I have provided basic references for readers who wish to gain a deeper understanding of the scientific and the spiritual principles that relate to emotional management.

My greatest desire for readers is that they grow in their emotional intelligence skills and encourage responsible decision-making and strong personal and professional relationships among all socioeconomic classes. I hope this book serves as inspiration to readers to improve on what I have attempted to do and will become even more inspired to search for greater knowledge and continue to grow their interpersonal and professional relationship skills.

Part I

The Foundation:
Self-Awareness

Chapter 1

Life Story: The Police Shooting of an African American Male

This story begins one Friday afternoon in July 2016. Nancy and Alicia, her four-year-old daughter, and Michael, Nancy's fiancé, were driving home from Michael's job. He was a thirty-one-year-old African American who worked as a high school youth counselor. The entire family was in a very good mood. They had just stopped at an ice cream parlor in the neighborhood at the request of Alicia, who loved chocolate ice cream with nuts on a cone. Alicia was buckled in her seat in the back of the car. Nancy was driving Michael's car.

Nancy noticed in her rearview mirror a police car with flashing blue lights approaching her. She instantly became nervous and afraid because she was aware of how police officers typically responded to African American drivers in her neighborhood. She reached for her phone so she could have evidence of what happened. Michael also became nervous because police had stopped him many times. He had a gun, but he had a permit to carry it. The police officer approached the car on the driver's side. Michael informed the police officer that he had a gun and a permit to carry it.

The day ended with the police officer shooting Michael several times as Nancy videotaped her conversation with an obviously upset police officer. Alicia was screaming and horrified as she sat strapped into the backseat of the car as the police officer fired into the car and killed Michael.

I believe this is a classic example of poor decision making and poor social and emotional management skills. This story accentuates the importance of making good decisions and putting social and emotional skills into action. I believe that it is obvious to any fair-minded person that both the civilians and the police officer had a responsibility for managing their emotions and

1

making good decisions to reduce the chances of having an out-of-control incident as illustrated in this life story.

We will revisit this case after I present the foundation theory on emotional control. At the end of this chapter, I present the important lessons that this story illustrates.

Scripture

People with understanding control their anger; a hot temper shows great foolishness. (Proverbs 14:29)

A gentle answer deflects anger, but harsh words make tempers flare. (Proverbs 15:1)

Like a city whose walls are broken through is a person who lacks self-control. (Proverbs 25:28)

Fools vent their anger, but the wise quietly hold it back. (Proverbs 29:11)

Solomon's writings in Proverbs demonstrate self-discipline, self-control, and temperance. Readers familiar with the Bible will recall that King Solomon (King David of Israel's son) was the wisest man who ever lived. Therefore, these Bible verses have stood the test of time. The readers who are unfamiliar with the Bible will also recognize the importance of these verses for present-day living.

Scriptures show examples of how Spirituality has been used throughout the Bible to help individuals manage emotions and make better decisions.

Parable: Solomon Judges Wisely

Sometime later two prostitutes came to the king to have an argument settled. "Please, my lord," one of them began, "this woman and I live in the same house. I gave birth to a baby while she was with me in the house. Three days later this woman also

2

had a baby. We were alone; there were only two of us in the house. But her baby died during the night when she rolled over on it. Then she got up in the night and took my son from beside me while I was asleep. She laid her dead child in my arms and took mine to sleep beside her. And in the morning when I tried to nurse my son, he was dead! But when I looked more closely in the morning light, I saw that it wasn't my son at all."

Then the other woman interrupted, "It certainly was your son, and the living child is mine."

"No," the first woman said, "the living child is mine, and the dead one is yours." And so they argued back and forth before the king.

Then the king said, "Let's get the facts straight. Both of you claim the living child is yours, and each says that the dead one belongs to the other. All right, bring me a sword." So a sword was brought to the king.

Then he said, "Cut the living child in two, and give half to one woman and half to the other!"

Then the woman who was the real mother of the living child, and who loved him very much, cried out, "Oh no, my lord! Give her the child—please do not kill him!"

But the other woman said, "All right, he will be neither yours nor mine; divide him between us!"

Then the king said, "Do not kill the child, but give him to the woman who wants him to live, for she is his mother!"

When all Israel heard the king's decision, the people were in awe of the king, for they saw the wisdom God had given him for rendering justice. (1 Kings 3:16–28)

Chapter 1

What Is Emotional Intelligence (EI)?

Daniel Goleman popularized the term *emotional intelligence* (EI). In *The Brain and Emotional Intelligence: New Insight* (2011), he gave readers a summary of the three most popular models of emotional intelligence.

There are three dominant models of emotional intelligence, each associated with its own set of tests and measures. One comes from Peter Salovey and Jon Mayer, who first proposed the concept of emotional intelligence in their seminal 1990 articles. Another is that of Reuven Bar-on, who has been quite active in fostering research in this area. The third is my own model, which is most fully developed in *Primal Leadership*, a book I wrote with my colleagues Annie McKee and Richard Boyatzis.

This book uses Goleman's model of EI, which consists of four components or competencies as shown in table 1. He also presented four components and discussed them on two levels: the individual or self level and the other or social level.

Self-Awareness	Social-Awareness
Self-Management	Relationship Management

Table 1

The Individual/Self Level

The individual/self level of Goleman's model consists of self-awareness and self-management. This level is the beginning point for understanding and managing one's emotions. The model stresses the importance of understanding one's self and knowing the triggers that evoke certain emotions. An in-depth knowledge of one's self is the beginning of effectively managing one's emotions.

The Other or Social Level

The other or social level consists of social awareness and relationship management. It focuses on the emotions of others including understanding their emotional states.

> "Scientists describe the open loop as 'interpersonal limbic regulation,' whereby one person transmits signals that can alter hormone levels, cardiovascular function, sleep rhythms, and even immune function inside the body of another. This book's cover design captures this concept" (Goleman, Boyatziz, & McKee, 2002, p. 7).
> Internal brain functions and the external brain functions of others influence our emotions.

The emphasis is on spoken words as well as on unspoken words or nonverbal cues such as body language and facial expression. In *Primal Leadership*, Boyatzis, McKee, and I described the human brain as an open-loop rather than a closed-loop system. In describing how brain scientists characterize the open-loop function of the brain, we noted,

> Scientists describe the open loop as "interpersonal limbic regulation," whereby one person transmits signals that can alter hormone levels, cardiovascular function, sleep rhythms, and even immune function inside the body of another. The internal and external brain functions of others influence our emotions. From the description above, one can infer the importance of our emotions in interpersonal relationships. Interpersonal relationships and the concept of *the social brain* are the emphasis of interpersonal neurobiology, a relatively new area in brain research.

Researchers in this field are particularly interested in how mirror neurons function during interpersonal relations. (Goleman 2011)

This book gives practical examples of effective and ineffective emotional control. Interaction between individuals likely occurs via mirror neurons. A simple example is observing the reaction between two individuals in a negative situation and two others in a positive situation. In both situations, one will notice that speech patterns and body language are likely to be the same for both individuals. A simple strategy for handling a negative situation would be to lower your voice's volume and increase an open-body stance with neutral or friendly facial expressions.

A detailed explanation of mirror neurons is beyond the scope of this book. Interested readers can review the works of Dr. Daniel Siegel, director of Mindsight Institute at the University of California, Los Angeles (http://drdansiegel.com/). It is important to emphasize that one can benefit from scientific principles without having detailed knowledge of how and why the principles are effective in managing emotions.

Controlling Emotions versus Effectively Managing Emotions

Most normally functioning individuals can control their emotions in most situations, but that does not mean they can manage their emotions in the most effective ways possible. Effectively managing emotions requires a high degree of emotional intelligence. Effectively managing emotions means that one is able to manipulate oneself and the environment to get the desired results.

Returning to this chapter's life story, we find that black America is upset over Michael's death at the hands of a white police officer. The news points to a very disturbing trend.

NEW ORLEANS (AP) — shooting deaths of law enforcement officers spiked 78 percent in the first half of 2016 compared to last year, including an alarming increase in ambush-style assaults like the ones that killed eight officers in Dallas and Baton Rouge, according to a report released Wednesday.*

The conflict between police officers and black Americans has increased particularly in urban areas. What can we learn from this story? Four important issues immediately appear to most readers. One, strong feelings and emotions were present among all the individuals in this story. Two, emotions affected the individuals' perceptions of the facts of this story. Three, controlling one's emotions and managing one's emotions are not the same actions. Four, managing emotions means that one is able to accomplish the desired results while maintaining effective relationships with others.

Issue 1: Emotions Evoke Strong Feelings such as Fear, Anger, and Mistrust

Taking an in-depth view of issue 1 in this story, we find that African Americans in this particular socioeconomic environment have mostly negative feelings about police officers. Police officers' training instructors teaches them to respond in a cautious manner in certain high-crime communities. Often, the high-crime communities are African American communities. Police training sometime involves techniques that appear to African American as hostile and highly prejudiced against them.[1]

I included two articles written by law enforcement officers that presented excellent information that helps readers to better understand the possible influence that perception has on law enforcement officers' actions.[2] It is very important to understand the role of mirror neurons when a police officer interacts with a potential criminal. The officer's and the citizen's emotions are communicated to each other verbally and nonverbally. However, because of the highly charged emotional situation and past negative interactions, both parties will likely be under the influence of their social and environmental conditioning. I will in future chapters discuss and present scientific evidence to support how emotions affect perception and rational thinking.

---

* http://www.usnews.com/news/us/articles/2016-07-27/report-shooting-deaths-of-law-enforcement-spike-in-2016.

Issue 2: Emotions Affect the Individuals' Perception

This statement relates to findings about how humans make decisions quickly without much effort or conscious thought. I used two different but related scientific perspectives in this book to help readers understand this quick decision-making process. The first perspective is from Operant Behavioral Psychology. This involves past learning or past conditioning and stimulus generalization. The second perspective is an updated view that expands our understanding of what happens in the human brain/mind in what Dr. Siegel refers to as a **Top-down approach** to decision making vs. a **Bottom-up approach** to decision making. (Mind-Journey-Heart-Being-Human. Daniel J. Siegel, M.D. 2016)

An in-depth analysis of issue 2 in the story emphasizes how perception influences African Americans and particularly those who live in high-crime communities. Nancy's perception of what happened in the story was most likely significantly different from the police officer's perception of what happened. According to the Gallup Review, black and white views toward police officers are significantly different.[3] African Americans consistently rate police officers in a more negative way when they interact with police officers and the American justice system. White Americans consistently report a more positive view of their interaction with police officers. This finding does not surprise me as it is very consistent with my personal experience as an African American male, and it is consistent with the science on human behavior. I will discuss this in the remaining chapters of this book as it was one of my major objectives in writing it. I will emphasize that this is not a negative or a bad side of human nature but a natural one and can be a very positive aspect of human behavior.

Issue 3: Controlling One's Emotions and Managing One's Emotions Are Not the Same

Nancy, Michael, and the police officer were very much in control of their emotions; Nancy and Michael were attempting to comply with the officer's request to stop and present the information the officer requested. If Nancy and Michael had not been in control of their emotions, they would have overtly attempted to resist the officer and not comply with his request. That did not happen; that was obvious based on the videotaped conversation between Nancy and the police officer immediately after the shooting occurred. However, it is not completely clear who was managing his or her emotions effectively.

There were some questions about when exactly the police officer shot Michael. Two officers made the stop. The second officer was on the right side of the car and had full view of Michael's actions. That officer never drew his gun. Why did the officer on the driver's side pull his gun and shoot Michael? It is clear that he did not instantly shoot Michael as he approached the car. That indicated he was in control of his emotions.

In the videotape, it appeared that Nancy was managing her emotions in that she attempted to achieve the desired results—to keep her child in the back seat safe and maintain a relationship with the officer who had just shot Michael so she could collect video evidence that would prevent this from happening to others. She did not attack the officer but kept trying to make sense of why the police officer had shot Michael while he was attempting to comply with his request.

The police officer appeared to be very upset and yelled at Nancy that Michael should not have reached for his gun. Nancy repeatedly told the officer that Michael had told him that he had a permit to carry a gun and that he was reaching only for his wallet when the officer shot him.

From the operational definition of what effective management of emotions entails, it is clear that Michael's actions and the police officer's actions do not match this definition. Michael's and the officer's desired result was to be safe; it is obvious that the police officer's desired result was not to shoot Michael. The important questions to consider are, What happened that caused Michael's death? Did the police officer fail to carry out his duties properly? Did Michael's actions cause the officer to shoot him? The answer to the first question is not likely as simple as many readers who either blame the police officer or blame Michael for his own death would claim.

It has been over a year since this incident occurred. A jury acquitted the police officer of all charges related to Michael's death, which did not surprise African Americans. The city officials took action to remove the police officer from his job by offering him a voluntary separation agreement. The city issued a statement: "The public would be best served if the officer were no longer a police officer in our city." This case is an example of why the high level of distrust in African American communities of local law enforcement continues. The biggest issue for law enforcement officials is controlling crime in urban areas while maintaining trust with residents. Controlling crime and maintaining trust are not mutually exclusive as some believe.

Issue 4: Managing Emotions Leads to Our Desired Results while Maintaining Effective Relationships with Others

What follows is an in-depth view of this story with issue 4—effectively managing one's emotions to achieve the desired results. This life story is a classic example of where effectively managing emotions did not occur. Police officers who shoot others do not do so because they desire to do that but because they want to protect themselves and others and prevent crime. However, to ignore individuals' perceptions of the story in light of what science and spirituality tell us about people's perception is not wise.

I will give a brief overview of the basis for using both science and spirituality in effectively managing emotions. Following the brief overview, I will introduce the remaining chapters in this book in which I give short discussions of each chapter's key emotional management topics. I hope that readers will find this overview helpful in quickly finding topics of interests.

Using Science and Spirituality to Manage Emotions

Advances in the neurosciences, epigenetics, and other related sciences have made giant leaps in helping us understand emotional management. I present examples of these advances in this book. There is a growing trend and a general understanding that spirituality plays a significant role for many individuals in their efforts to manage their emotions. I present examples of scientific research lending strong support to the efficacy of using both spirituality and science in helping individuals manage their emotions. My personal life story of using science and spirituality in effectively managing my emotions serves as personal validation. In chapter 5, I present incidents from my life in which emotional management was a life-or-death situation. I discuss my struggles in effectively managing my emotions in a combat zone. I also discuss learning to manage my emotions and having cancer while being a caregiver to my wife, who also has cancer.

It might not be obvious to some readers why emotional management is so important. Most humans have a strong desire to have a sense of being in control of what happens to them. When we lose this sense of control, we feel not in control of our emotions and we feel behavioral and psychological dysfunction. Readers will discover that the human brain's main functions are to support life's biological functions and mental and metacognition (the ability to think and to think about thinking) functions. In addition, it is important for readers to know that the brain and the mind are not the same as the mind can control the brain.

Some writers closely associate the mind with spirituality. The brain and the mind function to get a person into a state of well-being in which the mind, brain, body, and spirit are harmonious. Ineffective emotional management leads to disharmony. This becomes evident by conflict among individuals, dysfunctional behavior, unhealthy stress, and even physical sickness. I have included some of the most recent research findings from the Benson-Henry Institute for Mind Body Medicine site.[4]

Quick Summary of this Book's Contents

Part I: Self Awareness

Chapter 2 gives a fictional characterization of two children who were unable to control their emotional impulses when it came to eating marshmallows. The study compared groups of children with two types of incentives; the first was to receive one marshmallow immediately, and the second was to receive two or more marshmallows if they wait and delayed gratification until the experimenter came back to the room.

This chapter reviews the original marshmallow experiment conducted at Stanford University in 1972 (Mischel, Ebbesen, and Zeiss 1972). I discuss the significance of the marshmallow study and present the updated findings from a selected sample of participants in the original study.

In chapter 3, I examine more closely some reasons that some of the children were not able to delay their gratification. I use two fictional parental role models to emphasize the parents' roles in teaching their children social-emotional behaviors such as delaying gratification. I discuss two scientific approaches in shaping social-emotional learning: behavioral modeling and mirror neurons' influences in social behavior change. I offer my opinion about the possibility of neuroplasticity occurring during prolonged video game playing or excessive hours of watching negative television programs. I explain my opinions by presenting the conditions under which neuroplasticity occurs. In addition, appendix C gives comical ways of explaining neuroplasticity.

Part II: Social-Emotional Awareness

In chapter 4, I discuss external environmental factors that likely influenced the marshmallow eaters and their parents. Chapter 4 discusses community forces that influence the development of emotional control in children. In this chapter, I present a simple way to help readers understand the complex nature of emotional control. Readers can form a visual image of emotional control development and emotional management development. (Please refer to figure, ECD, in chapter 4).

Chapter 4 also helps readers understand how social forces contribute to or inhibit individuals' emotional control. It discusses the three major factors of emotional development.

1. individual genetic makeup, which is most easily understood as one's temperament or personality (Goleman 2004)
2. community forces such as school, peers, social class of parents, and political and economic forces
3. spiritual and religious views that shape values, morals, and beliefs.

I present evidence that helps readers understand that the first two factors of temperament and community influence the third factor, spirituality.

Managing one's emotions is never a purely rational process since emotions are usually the result of cognitive processes that one has limited awareness of and limited control over.

This chapter introduces some recent findings in neurobiology on the subject of the brain versus the mind as it relates to emotional control. I conclude chapter 4 by discussing how one's spiritual beliefs can help individuals manage their emotional impulses. I also emphasize that a spiritual solution based on solid scientific principles leads to effective management of emotions.

Chapter 5 presents suggested strategies for effectively managing emotions. I present strategies for managing one's emotions using three approaches. The first is a purely rational, scientific approach. The second is a purely biblical or spiritual approach. The third is a synthesis of the first two approaches.

The scientific strategies I use throughout this book include behavioral psychology, cognitive psychology, positive psychology, mindfulness, and other related therapeutic approaches. They are the foundation for the suggested strategies for teaching individuals how to manage their emotions. I present examples from the lives of three world-known spiritual leaders who used their emotional management skills to make important social justice changes to their countries and the world—Dr. Martin Luther King Jr., Nelson Mandela, and Mahatma Gandhi.

Part III: Self-Management

In chapter 6, I discuss my personal faith in action and provide examples of my use of spirituality and science to manage my emotions. I discuss how the spiritual approach described in this book is different from a religious approach in that I do not attempt to specify a particular religious belief; instead, I simply recognize the role an individual's beliefs and values in conjunction with his or her mind and brain has in managing one's emotions.

Combining the scientific with the spiritual approach results in a synthesis that recognizes how the mind can shape and change the brain;

with appropriate training and self-awareness, individuals can gain more control over their minds and emotions.

In chapter 7, I continue the discussion on the importance of using both science and spirituality to increase the likelihood of living a good life. I open the chapter by presenting the life story of two people whose lives demonstrated the synthesis of spirituality and science to achieve well-being in their lives. This chapter discusses the benefits of believing in spirituality and science from the perspectives of physical, emotional, mental, and spiritual well-being. It presents a scientific perspective on how to make faith real. Of course, I take issue with the idea that one needs science to make one's faith real. Throughout this book, I have presented the argument that one must have faith to exist; it is a matter of in what or in whom you have faith or belief.

Part IV: Emotional Management and Greater Decision-Making Efficacy

Chapter 8 presents four techniques to help readers assess their effectiveness in managing their emotions. The four assessments are of the 360-degree multiple-rater format as one's opinion of oneself is often inaccurate (Goleman 1986; von Hippel and Trivers 2011).

The first technique involves assessing your belief about how well you manage your emotions. The second technique requires examination of improvements in your personal relationships with others. The third technique involves assessing your professional relationships with bosses, peers, and subordinates. The fourth technique involves examining your leadership abilities as a member of your community, city, state, or country.

Chapter 8 ends with a discussion on how to grow from being good at managing your emotions to becoming excellent at that task, and it discusses many of the benefits of doing that. I suggest a total system based on my experience and research on how to achieve a life that has purpose and a sense of well-being. Chapter 8 ends with a suggested system of continuous self-development using a proven behavioral social learning model developed by Goleman and associates.

Chapter 9 summarizes the major points of this book and updates findings from the research discussed in chapters 1–8. The summary includes reminders of how the major points are currently used. I discuss how writing this book has inspired me to continue learning and applying the principles and techniques to help others to live well. I discuss possible uses for this book and predict implications based on the collaborative efforts of brain researchers and spiritual leaders.

My vision is one of great hope and optimism about the application of knowledge to achieve a greater understanding of how the brain, mind, soul, and body interact to achieve individual and societal well-being. Writing this book has reaffirmed my personal passion for serving others. I believe the key to living with real purpose, peace, and self-worth is serving others.

Life Story: Henry Robinson, Sixth Grader

The story begins at an after-school tutoring and mentoring session with Henry Robinson, a sixth grader. He lives at home with his mother; his father lives elsewhere. Henry is a very active and popular young man, but his popularity is problematic in that he loses focus on his homework.

His school counselor gave me a profile of Henry and a plan she suggested Henry and I work on during our mentoring sessions. The counselor informed me that Henry was behind in all his classes and that she was very concerned he would fail sixth grade.

As I became more familiar with Henry, I discovered that he had developed some very poor study and sleep habits. I also discovered that he did not have parental supervision immediately after school or anyone to help him with his homework at home. His poor sleeping habits were causing him serious problems with his ability to concentrate during our tutoring sessions.

During our casual conversations, I learned that Henry either played video games or watched television each night until he fell asleep. When I asked him what his bedtime was, he looked puzzled and said, "I don't know."

Henry's story continues at the end of this chapter.

Scriptures

These are the proverbs of Solomon, David's son, king of Israel. Their purpose is to teach people wisdom and discipline, to help them understand the insights of the wise.

Their purpose is to teach people to live disciplined and successful lives, to help them do what is right, just, and fair. These proverbs will give insight to the simple, knowledge and discernment to the young. Let the wise listen to these proverbs and become even wiser. Let those with understanding receive guidance. (Proverbs 1:1–5 NLT)

Direct your children onto the right path, and when they are older, they will not leave it. (Proverbs 22:6)

Parable of the Lamp

Then Jesus asked them, "Would anyone light a lamp and then put it under a basket or under a bed? Of course not! A lamp is placed on a stand, where its light will shine. For everything that is hidden will eventually be brought into the open, and every secret will be brought to light. Anyone with ears to hear should listen and understand." Then he added, "Pay close attention to what you hear. The closer you listen, the more understanding you will be given[c]— and you will receive even more. To those who listen to my teaching, more understanding will be given. But for those who are not listening, even what little understanding they have will be taken away from them." (Mark 4:21–25)

I will relate the chapter's scriptures and biblical parables at the end of this chapter.

Chapter 2

Meet Jack and Polly, the Marshmallow Eaters

As mentioned in chapter 1, in 1972, researchers at Stanford University conducted a landmark study exploring differences between children who chose to have one marshmallow immediately rather than waiting and receiving two or more marshmallows later.

Jack and Polly are siblings who live in Happyville; they represent children who would most likely choose to eat one marshmallow right away rather than delay gratification and receive two or more marshmallows later.

In this chapter, I explain the rationale for using the research findings from the famous marshmallow study to help explain emotional control as well as how genetic and environmental factors are involved in determining one's ability to manage emotions.

In chapter 3, I introduce Jack's and Polly's parents, and in chapter 4, I take an in-depth look at the community in which Jack's and Polly's family lives.

Polly, six, and Jack, five, are happy and well-adjusted children with no known physical or emotional problems. They enjoy the things and activities children their age typically enjoy. They spend a considerable amount of time watching their favorite television programs and playing video games.

Jack, a kindergartener, is learning the basics of getting along with other children and the fundamentals of reading. Jack's favorite part of the day is playing with other kids. He is also learning how to interact and control his emotions to please his teacher. He knows what the teacher expects by how she treats other kids who do not do what she expects. Jack is learning the rules of the classroom, but he has some difficulty with sharing. Jack's teacher constantly reminds him to allow other children to take their turns using the video controller to the classroom's gaming system. He often has mild temper tantrums and withdraws from playing with the other children when reminded to do so.

The grandparents always make sure Jack and Polly get the latest toys and games for their birthdays and at Christmas. Jack and Polly learned at an early age that if they wanted a new game or toy, they could always get it by asking their parents or grandparents. They have also learned that if their parents or grandparents say no to new toys or games, they can manipulate them into changing their minds.

The Manipulation Game

It is very important for parents and grandparents to understand the games that children will play to get what they want. Here we see Jack and Polly have learned at a very early age how to manipulate their family to get what they want.

Polly knows that if she looks sad or disappointed, her grandparents will give her what she wants. Jack in turn is learning how to use what Polly has gotten to get what he wants by saying, "That's not fair!" which typically prompts his grandparents to buy him a new toy or game as well.

The video games Jack and Polly play are all action oriented, which keeps them excited. The games also offer instant feedback about how well they are playing and give point rewards and more playing time as they get better at each skill level.

Some of the games, however, are not attractive to Jack and Polly particularly those that are difficult to learn or require many hours to gain skill in. They usually ask their parents to buy games that allow them to lower the level of difficulty so they can immediately receive the reward while playing the game rather than having to spend time learning skills before receiving rewards.

Jack really likes games that he can play by himself and that offer instant rewards. He also likes games that have his favorite television characters and allow him to listen or watch rewarding action while playing the game well.

However, Jack's parents are becoming concerned about his spending so much time playing video games and watching hours of television.

The friends Jack and Polly play with are very similar and engage in the same kinds of activities. The interactions among Jack, Polly, and their friends are mostly inside the home while playing video games or watching television. During the summer, they participate in some outdoor activities at the urging of their parents, but they are more attracted to computer and video games than to outdoor games, which do not offer them control or immediate rewards. The outdoor games are often stressful for the children physically and mentally.

Most of the children are physically out of shape because computer and video games do not provide physical exercise. Mental stress is high for many of them because most of the outdoor games are organized sports competitions that lead to perceived pressure from parents and coaches to win. This pressure is in addition to peer pressure and pressure the children put on themselves to measure up to their peers' performance levels.

Summary of the Original Stanford Marshmallow Study

The original marshmallow study was conducted by psychologist Walter Mischel of Stanford University (Mischel, Ebbesen, and Zeiss 1972). Its purpose was to examine cognitive and attentional mechanisms in delay of gratification. Three experiments involved three groups of preschool children ages three years and six months to five years and six months from the Bing Nursery School of Stanford University. The results of the three experiments were these.

Experiment 1 compared the effects of external and cognitive distraction from the reward objects on the length of time preschool children waited for the preferred delayed reward before forfeiting it for the sake of a less-preferred immediate reward. In accord with predictions from an extension of the frustrating nonreward theory, children waited much longer for a preferred reward when they were distracted from the rewards than when they attended to them directly.

Experiment 2 demonstrated that only certain cognitive events (thinking about fun things) served as effective distracters. Thinking sad thoughts produced short delay times as did thinking about the rewards themselves.

In experiment 3, the delayed rewards were not physically available for direct attention during the delay period and the children's attention to them was manipulated cognitively by prior instructions. While the children waited, cognitions about the rewards significantly reduced rather than enhanced the length of their delay of gratification. Overall, attentional and cognitive mechanisms that enhanced the rewards shortened the length of voluntary delay while distractions from the rewards overly or cognitively facilitated delay. The results permitted a reinterpretation of basic mechanisms in voluntary delay of gratification and self-control (Mischel et al. 1972, 204–18).

The marshmallow study was the basis for several follow-up studies that have helped explain the importance of one's ability to delay gratification and how this related to one's ability to manage his or her emotions.

The next section gives a brief summary of the findings of some of these studies and discusses some of the practical implications derived from the original marshmallow study's findings concerning delayed gratification and the possible links to managing emotions. Additional support from recent research in brain science (i.e., neurology and neurobiology) has influenced the interpretation of the findings from the earlier studies.

Updated Research Findings on the Subjects from the Original Stanford Marshmallow Study

Many studies followed up on the original Stanford marshmallow study test subjects, and I will briefly discuss two; they represent a sampling of some of the most interesting follow-up research in that these studies have important social and economic implications for why it is important to learn how to delay gratification and manage one's emotions.

Shoda, Mischel, and Peake (1990) conducted the first follow-up study; it examined the possible link between delay of gratification in preschoolers and later cognitive development as evidenced by the Adolescent Coping Questionnaire and Scholastic Aptitude Test (SAT) scores. In discussing the rationale for this type of study, the authors noted,

> To be able to delay immediate satisfaction for the sake of
> future consequences has long been considered an essential

achievement of human development. After a series of investigations into the individual differences associated with the choice to delay gratification ... research turned to the processes underlying the ability to sustain self-imposed delay of gratification after the initial choice has been made. (Shoda, Mischel, and Peake 1990, 978)

The ability to delay gratification is an essential component of human development. Moreover, research conducted by Shoda and colleagues (1990) supports the general conclusion that delaying immediate pleasure for more long-term benefits may lead to certain advantages in the future. Specifically, the preschool subjects from the original marshmallow study who were able to delay the immediate gratification of receiving one marshmallow in favor of receiving two or more marshmallows later were also able to make wise choices later in their teenage years especially those involving delay of immediate gratification.

In examining the results of Shoda (1990) in further detail, we see a statistically significant difference between subjects who delayed gratification at preschool age and those who failed to delay gratification at preschool age in terms of SAT scores, coping, and frustration tolerance. It was reasoned that the ability to delay gratification at an early age remains relatively constant as one becomes a teenager and throughout adulthood.

A Word of Caution

The reader should be careful when making broad generalizations from such a small sample of subjects selected from a very limited population as is the case with Shoda (1990). The study's authors caution readers in their discussion of the results and the nature of the long-term links, noting,

We must emphasize the need for caution in the interpretation of the total findings linking preschool delay to adolescent outcomes. This caution applies especially in the interpretation of the associations between preschool delay in the exposed-rewards-spontaneous-ideation condition and SAT scores. (Shoda et al. 1990, 985)

The researchers' caution in their interpretation of the results requires readers to make two additional observations. First, there was no way in this study to know what happened to subjects from preschool to high school that might have influenced their ability to delay gratification. The association between delayed gratification and SAT scores does not imply causation; many other factors could possibly have accounted for the association.

Second, it is a giant leap in logic to assume that if students can delay gratification, they will have higher SAT scores. The study's authors pointed out the need for additional research to get a better understanding of the mechanisms involved in delaying gratification and its long-term importance. The next section will discuss such a study.

Recent Study Forty Years after the Marshmallow Study

Casey et al. (2011) conducted the second follow-up study of interest; it examined sixty individuals from the original Stanford marshmallow study as well as related studies spanning forty years. The study examined the neural basis of self-regulation in individuals from a cohort of the preschoolers involved in the marshmallow study four decades previously. This study is very important since the researchers use actual brain scan technology (i.e., functional magnetic resonance imaging—fMRI—to study the subjects' brains. The fMRI technology allows researchers to identify specific areas in their brains that were activated during the trial.

Study Results and Discussion

In the Casey et al. (2011) study, researchers placed subjects in two experimental groups and performed two experiments. To make the experiments more age appropriate, the researchers changed the subjects' task from choosing to receive one marshmallow now or two marshmallows later to making gender discriminations between faces as well as discriminating between faces that were either happy or fearful. In experiment 1, subjects performed a cool version of a go/no go task. A cool go/no-go task has less salient qualities and is less likely to activate certain areas of the brain. In this experiment, the cool stimuli were neutral male and female faces. During the go task, subjects were to press a button when shown target faces. During the no-go task, subjects were instructed to withhold the button and then press for the nontarget faces.

In experiment 2, subjects performed a hot version of a go/no-go task. Hot go/no-go tasks have very potent qualities and are very likely to activate certain brain areas. In the hot go and no-go tasks of experiment 2, subjects had to discriminate between happy and fearful faces again by pressing or withholding buttons.

The results of the cool go/no-go tasks conducted in experiment 1 did not reveal any significant differences between the subjects who had been able to delay gratification in preschool and those who had not been able to do that. Conversely, the results of the hot go/no-go tasks in experiment 2 revealed that subjects who were able to delay gratification as children were also able to exert more self-control in the task of identifying happy and fearful faces.

Is There a Difference in Brain Scan of Preschoolers Who Delayed Gratification versus Those Who Did Not?

The Casey et al. (2011) study suggests three significant findings that support previous research on delay of gratification. First, resistance to temptation originally by the delay of gratification task and in the present study by a hot version of an impulse control task is a relatively stable individual difference. Second, consistent with delay experiments on the value of cooling the hot features of temptations, behavioral correlates of delay ability involves cognitive control in general and response to positive compelling cues in particular.

Third, resisting temptation is supported by ventral front striatal circuitry with the inferior frontal gyrus showing lesser recruitment in low delayers and the ventral striatum showing exaggerated recruitment in low delayers when resisting alluring cues. Overall, these findings suggest that sensitivity to positive social cues influences an individual's ability to suppress thoughts and actions and thus can undermine self-regulation.

This study lends much scientific support to the idea that the so-called willpower to resist temptation may not be equal for everyone; it suggests that a neurobiological component is involved in one's ability to resist temptation. In commonsense terms, peoples' brains are different and these differences can have an effect on peoples' ability to delay gratification as well as manage their emotions.

This study also suggests that certain environmental cues are more likely to influence the so-called hot tasks more so than the cool tasks. This finding is very important in helping determine what strategies are likely to be effective for a particular individual with a particular type of brain. It may seem difficult to tell what type of brain a person possesses, but an individual's temperament or personality provides very strong clues as to what type of brain the person has. I will discuss these issues in chapters 4 and 5 of this book.

Henry Robinson's Life Story Continued

Henry's life story is very similar to the chapter's fictional characters who live in Happyville. The major differences are in social and emotional environmental factors; I will discuss the environmental factors in chapter 3. The findings of the marshmallow studies present compelling evidence that the complex nature of delaying gratification is related to the ability to manage emotions.

Henry's poor study habits were related to his excessive television watching and video gaming, poor sleeping patterns, and the lack of paternal supervision at home. The consequences for Henry were very unpleasant and led to many dysfunctional behaviors, poor academic performance, and emotional and social problems at school and in his community. These consequences were immediate and obvious for those who knew and cared about Henry's well-being. What should those who were concerned about Henry have done?

A general approach to handling Henry's situation involved working with parents, teachers, counselors, and mentors to provide a supportive and structured learning environment that would have led to his developing social, emotional, and academic skills development. Many schools have a proven record of using social-emotional learning in the classroom.[5]

The scriptures and the parable in this chapter give some excellent insight into how spirituality supports the above general approach for helping Henry's well-being.

The point is made in Mark 4:23–25.

> Then he added, "Pay close attention to what you hear. The closer you listen, the more understanding you will be

given—and you will receive even more. To those who listen to my teaching, more understanding will be given. But for those who are not listening, even what little understanding they have will be taken away from them."

In the parable of the lamp. Jesus, one of the greatest teachers in the Bible, expressed the importance of paying close attention and listening to the teacher. He also emphasized the danger of not listening and losing understanding. Regardless of one's beliefs about the biblical significance of Jesus's teaching or Proverbs, we can easily understand how following such advice would help develop good habits for living well.

Parents, teachers, counselors, and mentors who understand and accept such biblical teaching are more likely to model these types of attitudes and behaviors while interacting with students and others. Readers understand that behavioral modeling and social learning via mirror neurons unconsciously influence and in some cases change others' behaviors.

School and home environments that support positive spiritual teaching will have a greater chance of helping students develop positive habits essential for social, emotional, and academic development. Most readers will likely understand and agree with the above discussion based just on common sense without even examining the scientific evidence.

However, scientific evidence points to an even greater and more important question: What will the long-term influences of these types of factors in young subjects have on later development of their brains and effective emotional management? This chapter summary gives strong clues to this question.

Chapter 2 Summary

We now have a better understanding of Jack and Polly and some of the factors that influenced their choices in delaying gratification; it was not simply a matter of willpower. Based on research, we know that the specific nature of the stimuli or rewards had a major influence on their ability to delay gratification.

An important finding from the updated research discussed in this chapter is that an individual's brain biology plays a major role in his or her ability to delay gratification. This suggests that a simple explanation of why one child is able to delay gratification while another cannot is difficult to understand in terms of cause and effect. The environment has a significant impact on the individual's brain biology. Research findings appear to suggest that environmental factors can influence the brain's biology through what scientists call epigenetics and neuroplasticity. (Appendix A offers a more in-depth explanation of neuroplasticity and epigenetics.) A basic understanding of these two terms helps in comprehending how the brain works during social interactions and how this influences emotional management.

Additionally, recent findings from neurobiology research on neurogenesis and synaptogenesis is helpful in understanding what the future is likely to hold in terms of a better understanding of how the brain and mind function in managing emotions. Appendices B and C offer a comical scenario that will help readers develop a general understanding of how neuroplasticity works in our daily lives.

Chapter 3

Life Story: The Woodson Family

This life story is an example of parents' behaviors that are likely to influence positive effective emotional management skills development in their children.

Archie and Josie Woodson have been married for fifteen years and have three sons: James, who is thirteen, David, who is eleven, and Dewitt, who is eight. Archie is about to turn forty; he recently changed careers from being a police detective in a drug enforcement unit to being a PE teacher and football coach at a middle school. To make the career change, he had to go back to college and earn a teacher's certification. His undergraduate degree was in law enforcement, and he recently completed a master's in educational leadership while working at the middle school, where he is the assistant principal. Josie is also an elementary school teacher.

I have had the honor to act as an informal mentor and supporter of the Woodson family; I have observed their parenting styles and emotional management skills for the past fifteen years. I have watched the family go through some difficult but also some very positive times. I will highlight the positive aspects that this family has learned from its struggles.

Archie and Josie established the foundation for their emotional management skill development. The Woodsons learned additional emotional management skills via mirror neurons and behavior modeling by observing the emotional management habits of their many successful relatives.

During one of our recent conversations, Archie updated me on the progress of his job and family. He described the challenges of juggling so many roles as a new school administrator, father, husband, tutor for his sons, and community leader, but he was proud of his accomplishments and commented on how bright his future looked. His sons were doing well in school. He was honest about how structure at home and school was very important. He told me that he and Josie had to work together to prepare their children for many events at different times and places. He mentioned that he had to focus on one of his sons who was slipping in his homework. He talked about making sure his sons' clothes were ironed and ready the night before, imposing a strict after-school and weekend study time, and enforcing bedtime rules.

Archie and Josie parented in a disciplined but nurturing way. He set the example for his sons to be successful in school and their sports. Both parents' priority was academics first and sports next. Archie and Josie are their sons' greatest fans. They never miss a game even with their difficult schedules. They always give verbal praise and many times will have some external rewards to recognize their sons' achievements in academic and after-school activities.

The following scriptures relate to anyone who wishes to improve his or her emotional management skills.

Scriptures

Parable: A Father's Wise Advice

> My children, listen when your father corrects you. Pay attention and learn good judgment, for I am giving you good guidance. Don't turn away from my instructions. For I, too, was once my father's son, tenderly loved as my mother's only child. My father taught me, "Take my words to heart. Follow my commands, and you will live. Get wisdom; develop good judgment." (Proverbs 4:1–5)

A Father's Exhortation: Acquire Wisdom

> My child, listen when your father corrects you. Don't neglect your mother's instruction. What you learn from them will crown you with grace and be a chain of honor around your neck.

My child, if sinners entice you, turn your back on them! They may say, "Come and join us. Let's hide and kill someone! Just for fun, let's ambush the innocent! Let's swallow them alive, like the grave; let's swallow them whole, like those who go down to the pit of death. Think of the great things we'll get! We'll fill our houses with all the stuff we take. Come, throw in your lot with us; we'll all share the loot."

My child, don't go along with them! Stay far away from their paths. They rush to commit evil deeds. They hurry to commit murder. If a bird sees a trap being set, it knows to stay away. (Proverbs 1:8–16)

Chapter 3

Meet Jack and Polly's Parents, Who Taught Them about Eating Marshmallows

Jack and Polly's parents are from Generation Y. Both are college graduates with very busy professional careers and involvement in their community. Michael is a supervisor for the fire department, and Susan is a CPA at an accounting firm. They have two children. Their demanding jobs require that they work at odd times during the week. They are often away from home at night, so they get childcare for Jack and Polly.

A Typical Week for the Marshmallow-Eating Family

A typical week for the marshmallow-eating family involves both parents working sixty to seventy hours per week and being away from home two nights per week on average. Jack and Polly enjoy having babysitters because they can usually get them to let them to do whatever they want as long as it is safe and consistent with their parents' instructions. They can watch TV or play video games while the babysitters do their homework.

When the parents are home, the family usually goes out to eat or has precooked food for dinner. Only on rare occasions do the parents cook and the entire family sits for a meal and talks. Susan and Michael are usually too exhausted from their demanding jobs to have time to fix a full meal for the family. Usually, once a week, the family goes to their favorite fast-food place for burgers and hot dogs; that is Jack and Polly's favorite night of the week.

Jack and Polly are very involved in extracurriculars; Polly takes violin lessons, and Jack usually plays soccer or Peewee football. That puts additional stress on Michael and Susan because they have to get them to and then home from these events.

When Susan and Michael are not busy with their jobs or with doing things for Polly and Jack, they watch TV and play video games. They spend most of their free time catching up with prerecorded TV programs or surfing Facebook or Twitter.

Parents transmit Habits to Their Children Via Social Behavioral Modeling and Mirror Neurons

Television and video games habits were likely transmitted to Polly and Jack via social learning and mirror neurons. This probably contributed to Polly and Jack's difficulties in delaying gratification since their environment conditioned instant gratification over their entire young lives. This also likely affected their brain structures through neuroplasticity.

How Did Jack and Polly's Parents Teach Emotional Control?

Susan and Michael transferred their habits to their children via social learning and mirror neurons. This probably contributed to Jack's and Polly's difficulties in delaying gratification since their environment conditioned them for instant gratification over their entire young lives. This also likely affected their brain structures through neuroplasticity. That is my opinion, but there is growing evidence to support it. Time and more research will prove if it is correct.

Research is clear on the effect of behavioral modeling in areas such as good reading habits for children whose parents are persistent readers. Research supports the claim that parental reading and behavioral modeling factors leads to academic success in the lives of children of such parents (http://www.michigan.gov/documents/Final_Parent_Involvement_Fact_Sheet_14732_7.pdf).

I resume the discussion on parental influence on children's social and behavioral actions in chapter 5. There is strong agreement that parents play a major role in their children's development and have a major influence on their children's later successes or failures. This simply means that parents' involvement with their children is very necessary for their success; however, parental involvement is not in itself sufficient. Other factors in the community and general environment are at work and are sometimes beyond the parents' control. Parents only share in the responsibility for their children's success or failure particularly in the early stages of their children's development (http://www.ncbi.nlm.nih.gov/pmc/articles/PMC2973328/).

We can say that parents' behavioral modeling influences their children's ability to delay gratification. Additionally, we know that delayed gratification is important to many other socially desirable behaviors. However, it is not clear as to the strength of parental influence in delaying gratification. The reader should exercise caution when inferring any direct causal link between parental behavior modeling and later life social behavioral demonstrations on the part of their children. To take a causal link view would be too simple and would miss the biology or genetic link and social environmental influences between parents and the child's later life behaviors. Taking an extreme view of the parents being totally responsible for the child's later actions, or taking the opposite extreme view of the parents bearing no responsibility for the child's later actions is not appropriate in either extreme case. Parents share in the responsibility for their children's later actions, but are not completely responsible for them.

We return our discussion to the opening chapter story of the Woodson family, which is a real story, it is an example of what the fictitious marshmallow eaters parents' and Henry's parents from chapter 2 could have done differently to improve their parenting and emotional management skills.

In contrasting the two families' parenting skills that likely contributed to the most effective emotional management development in their children, I list and discuss the essential habits of effective emotional management.

Habit 1. Establish clear and positive expectations for children's behaviors that conform to moral principle values and accepted social and behavioral norms.

Parents must tell, show, demonstrate, and follow up to assure that their children clearly understand what the parents expect of them. The only way parents will ever know if their children clearly understand their expectations is if they consistently see them meeting their expectations. Anything less will lead to unmet expectations.

The Woodson children's parents modeled habit 1 to them. One example of establishing clear and positive expectation is spending at least forty-five minutes reading a book from the family suggested reading list each night.

Habit 2. Demonstrate what you expect by your actions as a parent.

Children will do what they see you do and are not likely to do what you say. You are their number-one teacher! This is particularly true when they are young. When you are too busy or too tired from juggling many different roles as parents, your children are still watching what you do and listening to what you say. One example of demonstrating what your expectations are, would be you as the parent routinely reading a book for forty-five minutes from the family reading list each night.

Habit 3. Establish a routine for verifying that your children are performing to your expectations.

Parents can do this in many ways; the Woodsons routinely help their children with their homework and talk to their children's teachers to gain an understanding of their children's progress.

Demonstrate and express your positive expectations about your children's performance on tasks they are responsible for, but do not make them feel you do not trust them to be responsible—trust but verify, but do so randomly.

Habit 4. Establish positive consequences for meeting expectations and negative consequences for not doing so.

Randomly praise your children for performing as expected; do not make praise the automatic result of performing as expected. When children do not perform as expected, take away some valued activity such as playing video games and make the expected performance a condition for playing video games in the future.

Parents must be prepared to deal with their children's negative reactions to losing privileges. The Woodson parents have mastered the art of parenting in a disciplining but nurturing way. They do not give in to their children's whining or crying because they know that enforcing rules is necessary for their children to establish positive habits.

I will discuss the basic scientific principles of forming positive and productive habits in chapter 6. Mastering how to form and maintain productive habits is essential to maintaining consistency in parenting.

Habit 5. Parents and other childcare providers must be consistent in practicing habits 1 through 4.

Forming productive habits is the most important skill to master in parenting and effective emotional management skills development. I will give a detailed discussion of the power of habits as defined by Charles Duhigg in chapters 4 and 5 of this book. The only way to develop any habit is by repeating the process of cue–routine–desired reward. This series of steps occurs many times before they become part of our unconscious memory, but then it becomes a learned conditioned response that allows us to perform the action without consciously thinking about it. We learn this way, and most of our important daily actions occur this way. This is why it is so important for parents and their children's caregivers to be consistent daily with habits 1 through 4.

Habit 6. Demonstrate by your actions that you love and care for your child's well-being.

This chapter's scriptures and proverbs point out how important spirituality is in parenting and emotional management skill development. The Woodson parents grew up in Christian churches in which the book of Proverbs was part of their Sunday school and Bible study lessons.

"The Father's Wise Advice" as discussed in chapter 4 of Proverbs became a habit for the Woodson parents. Archie's early childhood education had a strong Christian teaching focus. He has managed to position himself in job settings in which the culture of the jobs had a strong Christian focus. This was true for the police department as well as his current job as a school administrator. Archie's conditioning has naturally made him a father who gives wise advice and always acts with his family's well-being as his greatest focus.

In summarizing chapter 3, it is important to return to the opening thought about parents' responsibility for teaching their children about delaying gratification. Proverbs reminds readers about the parents' responsibility to teach children when they are young so they can develop wisdom for the adult years. As implied earlier, teaching children at an early age to avoid instant gratification will not guarantee they will be able to do that throughout their lives. Mirror neurons play a role in transmitting certain cues that can influence learning and brain development. However, there is disagreement about the role of mirror neurons and emotional management.[6]

In the next chapter, we will examine some of the marshmallow community and discuss the interaction of the community's economic, social, and political forces on parents' effectiveness in teaching social-emotional skills to their children.

Part II

Social-Emotional Awareness

Chapter 4

Life Story: Igor Gomez, the Happy Millionaire

I had the pleasure of meeting Igor in an interfaith book club. He is a very likeable person from South America. He speaks five languages and has traveled and worked in many countries. I wrote about Igor because I have carefully observed and been mentored by him for five years, and he is my friend. I have observed his personality in many settings. We have worked collaboratively on consulting and business projects that involved leadership development, team building and relationship development, and financial education.

Igor's story represents an excellent example of someone who effectively manages his emotions. His life align well with the definition I have adopted in this book for someone who is managing his emotions well. In addition, his behavior that I have observed over the last five years reflects Richard Davidson's advice about when should one consider changing his personality traits/emotional styles.

Igor's dominant personality traits using the Big Five are extraversion and contentiousness. His dominant personality traits using the Florence Littuaer Personality Plus Model are sanguine and choleric. For readers who are unfamiliar with these personality types, I present examples of Igor's behaviors that mirror these descriptions. Igor is very outgoing and talkative. You could easily pick him out in a crowd because he is very friendly to everyone and considers no one a stranger. He loves meeting and talking with others. He always has a big smile and a friendly open stance that invites others to engage in a conversation. He is likely to be the first to speak when meeting for the first time. He is likely to have a book that he has authored or is currently reading and eagerly shares the book's contents. He has a habit of giving total strangers copies of his books. I have observed him on many occasions meeting strangers. During these meetings, he usually gets to know intimate details about the person within minutes. These are his positive extraversion and sanguine personality traits.

Igor is extremely task oriented and focused on accomplishing his goals. He keeps daily records of his personal and professional spending, and he tracks how well he is accomplishing his goals. He once told me that one of his goals each day was to meet three strangers and get to know them. He structures time to be with his family members, who live in North and South America. He is very careful to work with customers in his city, customers in other states, and customers in foreign countries. He has over a million online personal and professional contacts he communicates with daily online. He recently shared with me how he has changed his sleeping patterns to communicate with his personal and professional contacts in different time zones. The above are some examples of his positive temperament, personality traits, and behaviors.

The question that some readers might ask about Igor: How is his sense of well-being? This is a very personal question, only Igor knows the answer. However, if one would examine typical indicators such as his standard of living and the quality of his life, one would conclude that he is living well. I will return to the chapter's life story at the end of this chapter.

Scripture

For the love of money is the root of all kinds of evil. And some people, craving money, have wandered from the true faith and pierced themselves with many sorrows. (1 Timothy 6:10)

The Parable of the Shrewd Manager

There was a certain rich man who had a manager handling his affairs. One day a report came that the manager was wasting his employer's money. So the employer called him in and said, "What's this I hear about you? Get your report in order, because you are going to be fired."

The manager thought to himself, "Now what? My boss has fired me. I don't have the strength to dig ditches, and I'm too proud to beg. Ah, I know how to ensure that I'll have plenty of friends who will give me a home when I am fired."

So he invited each person who owed money to his employer to come and discuss the situation. He asked the first one, "How much do you owe him?' The man replied, 'I owe him 800 gallons of olive oil." So the manager told him, "Take the bill and quickly change it to 400 gallons."

"And how much do you owe my employer?" he asked the next man. "I owe him 1,000 bushels of wheat," was the reply. "Here," the manager said, "take the bill and change it to 800 bushels."

The rich man had to admire the dishonest rascal for being so shrewd. And it is true that the children of this world are more shrewd in dealing with the world around them than are the children of the light. Here's the lesson: Use your worldly resources to benefit others and make friends. Then, when your possessions are gone, they will welcome you to an eternal home.

If you are faithful in little things, you will be faithful in large ones. But if you are dishonest in little things, you won't be honest with greater responsibilities. And if you are untrustworthy about worldly wealth, who will trust you with the true riches of heaven? And if you are not faithful with other people's things, why should you be trusted with things of your own?

No one can serve two masters. For you will hate one and love the other; you will be devoted to one and despise the other. You cannot serve God and be enslaved to money. (Luke 16:1–13)

Chapter 4

Economic and Political Forces in the Marshmallow Community

The original marshmallow study occurred in a community with a specific set of environmental, economic, and sociopolitical forces. As is the case elsewhere, these forces had an influence on the lives of the parents and the children of the Bing Nursery School at Stanford. In this book, I created a fictional community, Happyville, in which Jack and Polly's family live.

> Decades of research have shown that both genes and environment work together in a complex tango of cause. This is the most accepted view, and helps with our general understanding of the role an individual's genetic makeup has in determining one's ability to manage his or her emotions. Both the environment and genetics interacts to form one's personality.

Families in Happyville in 2017 are very different from the families of the Stanford University community in 1972. This chapter discusses some of the most obvious differences between the Stanford study families and today's families in their ability to develop emotional control in their children. Specifically, this chapter explores the complex nature of human behavior and some of the forces that influence the development of emotional control. I discuss individual temperament or personality traits, and I examine community forces such as dominant political views, dominant social norms, economic conditions, and spiritual and religious views that shaped the values, morals, and beliefs of the families in the community.

Individual Temperament and Personality Type

Our unique genetic makeup, personality, and environmental conditioning determine our behaviors. Researchers have written extensively on how genes affect our personalities. In her book *Evil Genes: Why Rome Fell, Hitler Rose, Enron Failed, and my Sister Stole my Mother's Boyfriend*, Oakley (2007, 54) gives a generally accepted scientific view of how genes affect personality.

> Intriguing research has shown for example that abused boys who have genes coding for low levels of the enzyme MAO-A, which breaks down communication molecules in the brain, have a higher tendency to become violent or criminal than do other abused boys. When these children are raised in a normal environment, however, the gene does not appear to affect behavior. The low-coding MAO-A genes provided only a predisposition for antisocial behavior—an example of how both nature and nurture might combine to form personality as well as personality disorders.

It is beyond the scope of this book to give a detailed explanation of how genetics and environmental factors determine personality, but genetics and personality traits play significant roles in emotional management.

The Temperament/Personality Link

Researchers have studied how temperament and personality are related (Rothbart, Ahadi, and Evans 2000). A brief summary of this research is essential to understanding the nature and definition of personality.

The commonly accepted view is that temperament is strongly related to genetics and that individuals are born with certain predispositions to behave certain ways. Some researchers suggest that most of the dimensions in the big five factors of the personality model are associated with an individual's temperament.* Many of the theories on personality types came from research findings about temperament. I have provided references on the three most popular personality theories: the big five factors, the Myers-Briggs type indicators, and Florence Littauer's sanguine, melancholy, choleric, and phlegmatic types of personality (Costa and McCrae 1992; http://www. myersbriggs.org/my-mbti-personality-type/mbti-basics/; Littauer 1992).** A basic familiarity with these three models will help readers understand how someone's personality is an important factor in managing his or her emotions.

Emotional Control and Personality Type

Common questions about emotional control and personality type are: How does personality type affect my ability to manage my emotions? Can I change my personality type? Is there a personality type that is most helpful in managing emotions? Experts have studied these questions for centuries. Disagreement among experts on personality regarding the correct answers to these questions continues, but there are practical answers to each of these questions on which most experts tend to agree.

How Does Personality Type Affect the Ability to Manage Emotions?

Addressing this question requires an understanding of what is usually the accepted definition of an individual's personality from a commonsense perspective and a clinical or psychological perspective. The commonsense perspective involves looking at personality as "a dynamic and organized set of characteristics possessed by a person that uniquely influences his or her cognitions, emotions, and behaviors in various situations" (www.wikipedia. org/wiki/personality_psychology).

---

* The Big Five Factors are openness (inventive/curious vs. consistent/cautious), conscientiousness (efficient/organized vs. easygoing/careless), extraversion (outgoing/ energetic vs. solitary/reserved), agreeableness (friendly/compassionate vs. cold/unkind), neuroticism (sensitive/nervous vs. secure/confident; Wikipedia).
** Myers-Briggs Type Indicators: Wikipedia online gives an extensive review of this personality theory and how it correlates with other personality theories.

Personality involves one's way of thinking and feeling and the internal drives that influence how one would normally behave in a given situation. We can infer from this definition that trying to understand an individual's behavior based on his or her personality type is a complex process. Nevertheless, it is important to point out that personality type labels are widely used and very helpful in determining patterns of behavior in individuals as you will see from a clinical definition of personality.

A clinical definition of an individual personality is similar to the commonsense definition. The major difference is that in the commonsense definition, the emphasis is on communicating or describing how individuals routinely behave. In the clinical definition of personality, the major emphasis is on discerning a normal personality from an abnormal personality. The *International Encyclopedia of the Social and Behavioral Sciences* explains the clinical definition of personality this way.

> Personality, defined psychologically, is the set of enduring behavioral and mental traits that distinguish human beings. Hence, personality disorders are defined by experiences and behaviors that differ from societal norms and expectations. Those diagnosed with personality disorders may experience difficulties in cognition, emotiveness, interpersonal functioning or control of impulses. In general, personality disorders are diagnosed in 40-60 percent of psychiatric patients, making them the most frequent of all psychiatric diagnoses. (Saß 2001)

It is my desire that you gain a greater appreciation for personality as it is used in everyday conversation versus personality in its clinical sense. It is also important to understand that an individual's personality is very dynamic; many factors are at work including a person's environment. Therefore, making predictions based on personality requires a great deal of caution.

An example that illustrates this point comes from an employment selection process. Personality tests are invalid and unreliable selection instruments for making hiring decisions on future employees, so the law prohibits employers from using personality test results for selecting applicants without having valid data to support a significant relationship between the applicants' personality type and actual future job performance (Steingold 2003).

A person's personality interacts with other factors to control that person's emotions. Personality traits are key determinants to our everyday behaviors, so we can say that how well we manage our emotions is directly related to our personality type.

Most personality theories consist of individual temperaments. When we examine the various personality theories, we see that temperaments reflect traits and behaviors that influence emotional control (http://en.wikipedia.org/wiki/Temperament). This leads to the next question: can an individual change his or her personality?

Can an Individual Change His or Her Personality?

The current thinking on this question is that one can change his or her personality over time (http://www.huffingtonpost.com/2012/03/05/personality-change-over-time-study_n_1321720.html). Changing one's basic personality is much like what occurs in neuroplasticity. People can change their personalities, but that is not easy; it requires time and concentrated intentional effort or the appropriate environmental stimuli and conditions for this change to occur (http://en.wikipedia.org/wiki/Change_in_personality_over_a_lifetime).

Recent research in the neurosciences supports this opinion. The neurosciences have some very interesting findings on neuroplasticity and neurogenesis. In chapter 5, I will discuss neuroplasticity and neurogenesis and their roles in changing the brain.

Richard Davidson's research has taken a different approach to examining personality. He and his associates have discovered through their research that personality traits are related to emotional styles.

> Let me show, then, that Emotional Style has sufficient explanatory power to account for well-established personality traits and temperament types; later, particularly in chapter 4, we will see that it has a solid foundation in the brain, something other classifications scheme do not. (Davidson and Begley 2012)

Davidson has identified six emotional styles through his systematic study of the neural bases for emotions. Each of the six dimensions has a specific, identifiable neural signature—a good indication that they are real and not merely theoretical constructs. Each dimension describes a continuum. Some people fall at one or the other extreme of the continuum while others fall somewhere in the middle. The combination where you fall on each dimension adds up to your overall emotional style (Davidson and Begley 2012).

The following is a listing of the six dimensions of emotional styles. Chapter 5 will give an in-depth explanation of each with information from Davidson's research on how one can benefit from knowing about his or her emotional style. The dimensions of emotional styles include resilience, outlook, social intuition, self-awareness, context, and attention. A careful examination of these emotional styles will show the value of having a certain amount of each.

In *The Emotional Life of Your Brain*, Davidson and Begley (2012) give a concise explanation of at least two roles the environment has in shaping emotional styles. According to the authors, "The environment does not just shape behavior or even brain function. It also affects whether genes turn on or off and, therefore, which inherited traits we express" (112). It can be inferred that the environment is essential in changing the structure of the brain through epigenetics via neuroplasticity and that the basic genetic functions can be altered by the environment. Both of these conclusions about the environmental impact on personality traits and emotional styles are somewhat new and go against traditional thinking. However, Davidson's book does an excellent job of presenting research to support his findings on this subject. Now that we know we are not at the mercy of the personality we were born with, the question becomes, should we want to change our basic personality type?

There is a type of personality that is most helpful when it comes to managing emotions. There are obvious traits and temperaments that are more helpful in managing one's emotions than others. An interesting perspective Davidson and Begley (2012) present concerns determining when one's personality type or emotional style becomes a problem. According to the authors, a particular emotional style becomes a problem only when it causes difficulty for the individual.

> I support the belief that the most practical approach in managing emotions is to help individuals become aware of their dominant- personality traits or Emotional Styles and help them to understand the likely consequences of their behaviors in different environmental settings with different individuals that have varying personality traits and Emotional Styles. Once an individual gains this awareness, he can decide if his personality is problematic for him; then, and only then should one attempt to change his personality.

There is practical value in understanding this point. We are unique in our biological makeup and our environmental experiences. It is very difficult to pigeonhole people into specific behavioral patterns. There will always be variation along a continuum of traits or emotional styles for all. I support the belief that the most practical approach in managing emotions is helping people become aware of their dominant personality traits or emotional styles. Such awareness helps them understand the likely consequences of their behaviors in various environmental settings and with various individuals who have different personality traits and emotional styles. Once people gain this awareness, they can decide if their personalities are problematic. Only then should they attempt to change their personalities.

Davidson and Begley (2012) emphasize the idea that individual differences do not have to be a problem. In today's business world, diversity among individuals is desirable. Individuals can benefit by reframing their perspectives to see their unique personality traits and emotional styles as strengths rather than weaknesses that need changing.

In chapter 5, I discuss general positive personality traits and emotional styles that are likely assets for anyone in all situations. However, it is important to exercise caution when trying to make predictions about controlling one's emotions based solely on one's personality type or emotional styles. The next section gives brief examples of how community forces might influence emotional control in individuals.

Community Forces

Environmental factors have an influence on individuals' abilities to manage their emotions; they largely reflect the particular community in which the individuals spend most of their time. To describe a particular community, we need to examine factors such as the dominant social norms and political views and the dominant economic conditions of the community's members as these may very well vary widely. It is very difficult to make predictions about which personality types or emotional styles are best for managing emotions. Let us take a closer look at each of the community forces and examine them with these five questions in mind.

Five Important Questions:

1. What are the assumed dominant factors for each of the forces?
2. What do the extreme views on the high dominant side look like? What does the low dominant side look like?
3. Are there any real-world people who possess these extremes? How well do they manage their emotions?
4. How did they develop their emotional management skills?
5. How do interactions among dominant environmental factors, individual genetics, personality types, and emotional styles combine to determine how well one will manage his or her emotions?

Dominant Social Norms of the Community and Their Influence on Managing Emotions

What are the assumed dominant factors for each of the forces?

Community social norms are the beliefs, values, and morals commonly associated with most members of a particular community. The collective social views of each family in the community about its individual family values shape dominant social norms. Additional collective family social views that shape dominant social norms include beliefs about faith in a higher power, life after death, what is morally right or morally wrong, beliefs about the centrality of power, and the role of the government in one's personal life.

What do the extreme views on the high dominant side look like? What does the low dominant side look like?

To understand extremes in dominant views, let us compare someone who grew up in a family with a high dominant view about faith in a higher power with someone who grew up in a family that had a low dominant view about faith. The person who grew up with a low dominant view would likely have the views opposite to those of someone who grew up in a high dominant view.

Are there any real-world people who possess these extremes? How well do they manage their emotions?

I know many people who have been at these two extremes. I grew up in a family with very strong dominant views about the existence of a higher power. I know people who grew up in the same community who had a low dominant view on faith; however, this was not the prevailing view, the community norm. Unfortunately, it is somewhat difficult for me to determine differences in how well these individuals manage their emotions since I believe I am good at managing my emotions most of the time.

How did they develop their emotional management skills?

A strong moral or dominant faith view tends to help individuals have absolute beliefs about what is right and moral and what is wrong and immoral.

Many with high dominant faith views follow the teaching of a moral doctrine such as the Bible. It is important to note that I am not intentionally implying that those without a dominant faith view do not have a sense of what is moral or immoral. I believe that most humans have a kind of innate sense that leads them to know what is moral and immoral.

How do interactions among dominant environmental factors, individual genetics, personality types, and emotional styles combine to determine how well one will manage his or her emotions?

There are many possible explanations for how individuals develop their emotional management skills; I explore this in some depth in chapter 5, in which I show how I have developed my emotional management skills based on my experiences and background as a student of human behavior at four colleges not as a researcher but as someone who has helped shape the lives of many students. I also discuss how my industrial experiences working for three large American corporations and my service in the US Air Force during the Vietnam era have likewise shaped my knowledge on emotional management.

Beyond the experiences discussed above, I am the father of three who would make any parent proud. One of my children is a medical doctor, and the other two are business owners in the food-processing industry. My greatest joy and challenge has been trying to help them shape their lives so that they are happy, productive citizens. My academic background as a behavioral psychologist with an industrial emphasis keeps me stimulated and curious to learn something new about human behavior each day.

My environmental conditioning and my conscious and unconscious habitual behavioral choices have helped me achieve desired results and have led to the development of my emotional management skills. This may seem simple, but it goes much deeper than just looking at external stimuli, behavior, and consequences. Asking why humans behave as they do is quite different from asking why nonhumans do what they do. If it were true (as my behavioral psychology professors taught me) that there is no such thing as free will or choice, there would be no difference between humans and nonhumans; both would be doomed to their past conditioning and respond as a computer does to programmed codes of reinforcement and punishment.

There is much truth in the findings of operant psychologists (e.g., Ferster and Skinner 1957), but there is more to the story than the external stimuli view of behavior. As science has advanced, we now know that the mind can make choices different from expected behavioral responses to likely positive or negative consequences even when there is a behavioral history of responding a certain way based on certain external reinforcement and punishment.

Not all behavior is externally driven; the brain and the mind do not know the difference between external and imaginary stimuli. We know from sports psychology that when athletes practice their routine mentally without any physical practice, they improve their performance in actual competition (Waitley 1986). This is quite different from what was once assumed as the optimal way to learn a physical task (e.g., Allami, Paulignan, Brovelli, and Boussaoud 2008, Cisek and Kalaska 2004). Understanding how environmental factors, genetics, personality types, and emotional styles determine how well we manage our emotions therefore requires us to make sense of the interaction among all these factors.

The human brain, mind, and body make up a very complex integrated system that works interactively to manage emotions. Nevertheless, there is strong scientific evidence that supports the conclusion regarding question five. First, the body, brain, and mind influence personality development. There is much disagreement about how this happens or where the mind is physically located, but there is a commonly accepted premise that the mind, brain, and body interact to influence one's personality. Second, emotional styles relate to personality and can be specifically located in certain brain structures. Finally, genetics plays a major role in personality and emotional style development.

The environment is the common agent for the brain, the mind, and body. The human brain can constantly change by neuroplasticity as explained earlier. However, individual genes have a role through a process called epigenetic change, which refers to how genes are turned on and off by environmental conditions. Under appropriate environmental conditions and with qualified clinical help, individuals can target specific personality traits and emotional styles they wish to change. In some situations, these changes can occur as a natural consequence of environmental conditions that cause relevant genes to be on or off. In the case of neuroplasticity, this can occur from focused attention over time to rewire certain brain functions (Goleman and Davidson 2017). I will discuss this in chapter 5.

Dominant Political and Legal Views of the Community and Their Influences on Managing Emotions

What are the assumed dominant factors for each of the forces?

Another dominant force is the community's political and legal views whether liberal or conservative. Many times, community members disagree on political and legal views. Individual members within the same family may even disagree.

What do the extreme views on the high dominant side look like? What does the low dominant side look like?

If we consider the extreme views of say conservative political voters as the major dominant view versus the minor dominant view of liberal political voters, we can again get at how individuals are likely to think and feel about certain issues.

Are there any real-world people who possess these extremes? How well do they manage their emotions?

We all have examples of conservative and liberal extremes readily available through the media. I say that those on either extreme do not manage their emotions very well. This we observed during debates and arguments over legislation such as the Affordable Care Act.

Of course, they never thought they were not in control of their emotions; they blamed those at the other extreme. Nevertheless, the majority of Americans saw that both sides were out of touch with the people who had elected them. An example very similar to the above example is the 2016 presidential campaigning season and the election of President Donald Trump.

How did they develop their emotional management skills?

Answering that requires a great deal of sensitivity. How does one choose to become a politician? Looking at the personality types of presidents and famous leaders can be demoralizing or uplifting depending on your personality type. My personality type mirrors Barrack Obama's. When considering him, I am uplifted. Nevertheless, I have never had the slightest desire to run for any public office.

How do interactions among dominant environmental factors, individual genetics, personality types, and emotional styles combine to determine how well one will manage his or her emotions?

The environmental conditions in which politicians grew up will have a large influence on their emotional styles and therefore a strong effect on how they manage their emotions. Senators from very conservative or very liberal states are likely to manage their emotions to please their key voters because they want to be reelected. This then becomes the antecedent of a gradual personality and emotional style change occurring over time through the process of what I have coined environmental neuroplasticity and environmental epigenetic change. (This is my attempt at neuroscience humor). I think most rational individuals would agree that the environment politicians govern in gradually changes them the longer they are in office.

Economic Conditions of the Community and Their Influence on Managing Emotions

The economic conditions of any community is assessed by examining what economists and business writers refer to as the standard of living and the general quality of life in the community (Kelly, McGowen, and Williams 2014). The quality of life (QOL) and the standard of living (SOL) are significant factors in the overall well-being of families and individuals. These factors are essential environmental conditions involved in shaping one's personality and emotional styles.

From a commonsense approach, one can easily understand how the environments of two individuals are likely to be very different. One may have grown up in a home with two well-educated parents and a family income above the national average while another may have grown up in a single-parent home with a low family income. They are likely to have vastly different environmental histories that have a significant influence on how their personality traits and emotional styles developed as well as how they learn to manage their emotions. This will become even clearer as we continue to explore the answers to the five questions we have been examining for each of the community forces.

What are the assumed dominant factors for each of the forces?

How does being a member of a relatively affluent household influence someone's potential for managing emotions? Keep in mind that such families could also suffer from bad financial management habits and poor parenting skills (Brady and Woodward 2013). The extreme negative dominant force is likely to be the case for those in one-parent and low-income households. Of course, there are exceptions, but economic deprivation has complex and multiple adverse effects on social-emotional development (Eamon 2001, Wilkinson and Pickett 2015). This is very significant when we examine some of the more recent findings on the brain's roles in parent-child attachment and development.

What do the extreme views on the high dominant side look like? What does the low dominant side look like?

Using our above descriptions of high and low dominant economic factors, I first look at the high positive, individuals and families that are not economically deprived. One would expect them to have personality traits, emotional styles, and emotional management skills that most likely lead to a high SOL and a wonderful QOL, but this is at best a naïve guess and a serious error in assumption. It is much too simple and does not take in to account the actual person and his or her life narrative (Siegel 2010).

One would expect the opposite assumptions about the extreme negative dominant view individuals who grew up in economically deprived environments. Again, we need to know the specific individual and his or her perception or life narrative of what happened in his or her environment though research is very clear that growing up in economically deprived environments will likely have adverse effects on social-emotional development.

> The main purpose of this dialogue is to provide information to help readers understand that each individual is unique. I recommend that considerations based on group research findings should be used only when most appropriate.

Most social science research uses group data and routinely examines averages or consolidated responses. The studies' inferences about results reflect differences among group averages. However, in the real world of making a difference with individuals and families, it is always essential to understand the unique experiences of each individual and know how he or she thinks and interprets his or her world. My intention is not to imply that group data or scientific research on groups is unimportant; they are not, but each individual is unique and should always be treated as an individual with considerations based on group research findings when most appropriate.

Are there any real-world people who possess these extremes? How well do they manage their emotions?

We all know people from both ends of the extreme, and we can all think of examples of people with very high and very low SOL and QOL. The same applies to how well an individual from either side manages his or her emotions—we all know individuals from both sides who are skilled at managing their emotions and others who are not. Belonging to one end of an extreme does not automatically determine how well an individual can manage his or her emotions.

How did they develop their emotional management skills?

Most readers have likely figured out that emotional management skills are a combination of genetics, personality, and environment. I believe this is very empowering in that regardless of what has happened in the past, people can change how they interpret what happens in their lives and create more-desirable futures for themselves. The ability to do this is largely a factor of the life narratives individuals repeat to themselves daily. I will discuss this in more depth in chapter 5.

How do interactions among dominant environmental factors, individual genetics, personality types, and emotional styles combine to determine how well one will manage his or her emotions?

The answer to this question is very similar to the answer given for the other community forces.

Activity for Fun 1

Let us have a little fun. Pretend that you are taking a class to learn about how to have a happy life.

Your first assignment is to:

1. Interview ten different people who look and act as if they are very happy in life. Also, interview ten different people who look and act as if they are very unhappy in life.
2. Use the questionnaire in appendix F to do your interview and answer the questions after you have completed the interviews for both groups.

> – What was the common theme of the very happy people?
> – What was the common theme of the very unhappy people?
> – Which group appeared better at managing their emotions?

However, economic forces are at the core of the community factors. As we all know, a family's financial situation influences how much stress exists in that family. Economic deprivation evokes many environmental stressors for individuals and families, but economic abundance can also be a stressor depending on the individual's life narrative or perception. Environmental stressors combine with an individual's genetics and neuroplasticity to shape that individual's social-emotional life and influence how well he or she manages emotions.

Dominant Spiritual Views and Their Influence on Managing Emotions

One's spiritual/religious view sets the foundation for all the above factors. Therefore, it is important to answer each of the five questions for this section.

What Are the Assumed Dominant Factors for Each of the Forces?

The assumed dominant factor is one's strong or weak belief in the existence of God or a higher power. When people believe in a God or higher power that controls and sets their life purpose, this is the extreme high dominant view. When people doubt the existence of God who controls and sets their purpose, that is the extreme low dominant view.

What do the extreme views on the high dominant side look like? What does the low dominant side look like?

Many real-world people possess both of these extreme views. The extreme high dominant view individuals are likely to better handle very difficult and stressful situations such as medical and relationship issues than extreme low dominant individuals are. They are generally more hopeful and have a more positive outlook than extreme low dominant view individuals have. I will present research findings in chapter 5 that support the above statements. It is important to point out that some individuals from both extremes have difficulty managing their emotions.

Are there any real-world people who possess these extremes? How well do they manage their emotions?

As mentioned before, I possess extreme high dominant views on spiritual and religious views. I teach Sunday school at my church. Some of my students initially had extreme low dominant views when they started my class. My skills at managing my emotions continue to grow as I practice my faith daily, and my students also grow in their faith.

Extreme low dominant view people often doubt the existence of God and are likely to be what psychologists call extreme internal locus of control people. They believe they are totally in control of their lives by the choices they make or fail to make.

How did they develop their emotional management skills?

The possible answer to this question is that they do so by developing their emotional management skills based on social learning and mirror neurons. This explanation is true for me. My social learning about spirituality and religion began early in my life with my parents and my community members who had extreme high dominant views about religion, Southern Baptist to be specific. My parents took me to church on Sundays during my childhood. Using social learning and mirror neurons, I observed and imitated the religious services. In my teen years, I became involved in helping one family with a special-needs child and became emotionally involved in his care; that taught me a lot about empathy.

In my family and community, I observed many incidents of anti-religious behavior that caused me to question my views about spiritual and religious practices. I have made sense of why there were inconsistences among my parents and my community over the years in their spiritual and religious practices. I discuss my life story in chapter 5.

How do interactions among dominant environmental factors, individual genetics, personality types, and emotional styles combine to determine how well one will manage his or her emotions?

The answer is very similar to previous responses to this question. However, I have taken some advice from Jesus's teaching and used a parable to explain this interaction. My view is that genetics is the seed, that the dominant environment is the soil, and that personality and emotional styles produce the fruit of one's emotional management skills. This makes sense for me since I believe God has created the capacity for human genes to develop and be altered by environmental factors.

Personality and emotional styles are linked to brain structures. We also know via epigenetics that gene expression occurs with the aid of the physical environment. The interaction of the dominant factors above are collectively responsible for one's emotional management skills development. Without effective integration of the individual environmental dominant factor, there would be ineffective emotional management skill development. An analogy will make this clear. To make a delicious apple pie requires the careful and thoughtful mixing and the interaction of all its ingredients. This analogy is very true about our lives in that when we fail to achieve harmonious integration among the key internal and external dominant factors, our well-being suffers.

To summarize this chapter, I refocus the reader's attention back to this chapter's life story at the beginning of this chapter. As I discussed in this chapter, genetics as reflected in temperament, personality traits, and emotional styles combined with external environmental factor influenced his emotional management style. Igor's emotional management skills were effective, and he has a strong desire to live an exemplary life of excellence and well-being financially, spiritually, mentally, socially, and emotionally.

To help readers to get a better understanding of this, we will examine questions 2, 4, and 5 below relative to the external environments for Igor.

Dominant Social Norms of the Community and their Influence on Managing Emotions	Dominant Political and Legal Views of the Community and their Influence on Managing Emotions	Dominant Economic Conditions of the Community and their Influence on Managing Emotions	Dominant Spiritual/Religious Views and their Influence on Managing Emotions
Question 2: What do the extreme views on the high dominant side look like? What does the low dominant side look like? Igor grew up in a family with high dominant social views who had a very strong faith and a sense of strong moral values.	I am unsure about his early childhood dominant views. I am sure of his current political view as being conservative to moderate.	His early childhood was on a farm his parents owned; they were entrepreneurs. His parents had a very strong work ethic.	His early childhood exposed him to the Catholic faith.
Question 4: How did he develop his emotional management skills? A possible explanation for how Igor's dominant views influenced his emotional management skills development is that his views gave him a moral code of what was right and wrong, honest and fair when	A possible explanation for how his dominant views influenced his emotional skills development is via behavioral modeling. Igor has worked with and was mentored by at least two of America's top CEOs. Igor also routinely interacts with many CEO's, domestically and	A possible explanation for how his dominant view influenced his emotional management skills development involves mirror neurons and social learning. Igor related stories to me about how he has observed his family during his life being entrepreneur's farmers.	A possible explanation for how his dominant views influenced his emotional management skills development is that he attended church services with his family and observed his family interacting with the community. Our first meeting was in an interfaith church group, which consisted of a very

Dominant Social Norms of the Community and their Influence on Managing Emotions	Dominant Political and Legal Views of the Community and their Influence on Managing Emotions	Dominant Economic Conditions of the Community and their Influence on Managing Emotions	Dominant Spiritual/Religious Views and their Influence on Managing Emotions
interacting with others.	globally. He speaks five languages.		diverse group of individuals.
Question 5: How do interactions among dominant environmental factors, individual genetics, personality types, and emotional styles combine to determine how well one will manage his or her emotions? A possible explanation for how effective interaction among the three major factors lead to effective integration and effective emotional management skill development is directly reflected in how successful Igor has been in making sense out of what has happened and why it happened from the stories that he repeatedly tells himself. (Part 1)	Successful interaction among the three major factors occurs only when there is effective integration among the three major factors. The integration occurs when we repeatedly tell ourselves stories daily. When someone makes sense of the what and the why of these stories, he or she can effectively develop the skills to manage emotions. (Part 2)	Some behaviors and mental attributes are evidence of successful interactions and integration. I will list the mental attributes first then the behaviors. **Mental attributes:** (1) Thinking positive thoughts. (2) Thinking and evaluating your own thinking. (3) Learning to rephrase own thinking. (4) Being able to separate thinking from feeling. 5. Avoiding making excuses	6. Learning to identify the origin of fears. 7. Identifying cues that trigger negative thoughts and feelings. **Behaviors:** (1) Taking important actions even if you are afraid or unsure of yourself. (2) Engaging in behaviors that affect important tasks, relationships, and people in your life. (3) Avoiding getting involved in unimportant behaviors. (4) Being willing to try something new. (All these reflect Igor's mental attributes and routine daily observable behaviors.)

Table 1. External Factors That Influence Effective Emotional Management Skills Development, Igor Gomez.

Question 5 above offers a good summary of what it takes to develop effective emotional management skills particularly in Igor's case. The chapter's scripture and biblical parables are examples of basic moral foundation principles that have guided Igor as he accumulated his wealth.

Figure 4 visually illustrates how emotional control and emotional management develops.

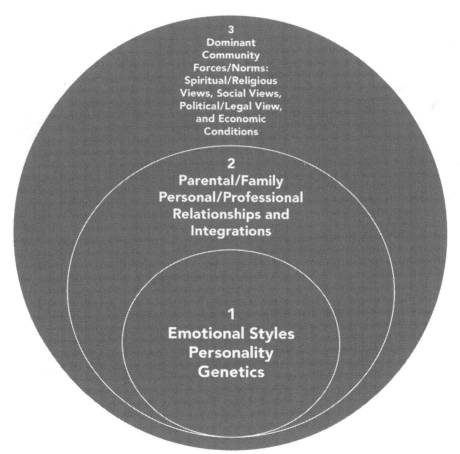

Figure 4. Model of Major Factors That Influence Effective Emotional Management Skills Development

Chapter 5

Life Story: The Minister and the Psychologist

A minister and a psychologist struggle to manage their emotions; they have experienced the pain of great loss and disappointment. I include this real-life story as an example of how science and spirituality have helped them effectively manage their emotions. I will offer a brief description of what had caused them pain, describe their key competencies, and discuss how they used those competencies to effectively manage their emotions. I will list some scriptures that they use to help manage their emotions.

One of them suffered from the suicide of a close relative early in his life, and the other lost two siblings and three other relatives in a car accident. They had been through divorces in which children were involved, but they maintained civil relationships with their children and their exes. They remarried, had more children, and were pursuing successful careers.

Key Competencies

The minister and the psychologist understand and practice scientific, psychological, and spiritual techniques for managing emotional conflicts. The minister has been a great mentor and spiritual counselor for the psychologist. The psychologist's life has been influenced greatly by listening to the minster's sermons and serving on his spiritual leadership team. Scientifically speaking, social learning and mirror neurons were involved in this influence process.

The two are natural teachers and love to help people live meaningful lives filled with a passion for a greater purpose. One is a national speaker and is very active locally and nationally practicing his craft and using his God-given talents.

One began his career at age eleven; he is now a senior citizen who still performs his craft. He understands and speaks Greek and Hebrew.

Both have advanced degrees and many years of experience in their professions; they believe in God and practice their beliefs; they teach Sunday school and Bible study.

Using Key Competencies to Effectively Manage Emotions

They understand the importance of forming productive habits that lead to effective emotional management. They routinely express the hot-button items that are likely to trigger major emotional outbursts in them, and they practice techniques for controlling or preventing that. They use their psychological training and empathy skills and demonstrate good listening skills.

One is very transparent about his struggles to control certain aspects of his life. They admit that both need divine guidance to help them deal with certain people and situations. They use prayer and scriptures to condition their minds and spirits to help them respond more appropriately and form productive habits.

Both are honest about how they still struggle with the loss of their loved ones at an early age. They have used their losses to help others deal with their loss of love ones as Christian church leaders, teachers, and friend to grieving individuals. They have accepted the fact that there are occurrences in life that makes no logical sense, but they rely on their faith to help them accept their losses. One of them often will remind himself of the scripture,

> "My thoughts are nothing like your thoughts," says the LORD. "And my ways are far beyond anything you could imagine. For just as the heavens are higher than the earth, so my ways are higher than your ways and my thoughts higher than your thoughts." (Isaiah 55:8–9 NLT)

He reminds himself that God's ways are superior to ours and that is why we must have faith. This scripture helps him reframe his life story so the tragic event that occurred in his early childhood makes sense to him. He often uses other scriptures to confirm and reassure himself that trusting God's words is the most important thing anyone can do.

The minister and the psychologist lean on the following scriptures to help them with life's difficulties and to remind them how they must act.

> Understand this, my dear brothers and sisters: You must all be quick to listen, slow to speak, and slow to get angry. Human anger does not produce the righteousness God desires. So get rid of all the filth and evil in your lives, and humbly accept the word God has planted in your hearts, for it has the power to save your souls.

> But don't just listen to God's word. You must do what it says. Otherwise, you are only fooling yourselves. For if you listen to the word and don't obey, it is like glancing at your face in a mirror. You see yourself, walk away, and forget what you look like. But if you look carefully into the perfect law that sets you free, and if you do what it says and don't forget what you heard, then God will bless you for doing it. (James 1:19–26 NLT)

Chapter 5 first presents scientific strategies for managing emotions. The second part of that chapter presents spiritual strategies for managing emotions. It is important to note that this chapter's life story applies to the second part of chapter 5 and chapter 6.

Chapter 5

Suggested Strategies for Managing Emotions

Chapter 1 introduced readers to the concept of emotional intelligence, EQ. We learned the importance of managing one's emotions rather than simply controlling them. I selected Goleman's (2011) model of EQ as the model of choice to explain emotional intelligence.

The personal and professional relationship among Goleman, Davidson, and McClelland helped our understanding of many proven strategies to manage our emotions.

The Power of Long-Term Relationships

David McClelland was a Harvard Industrial psychologist. He mentored both Daniel Goleman and Richard Davidson.

Goleman and Davidson are friends, and have a long history of being associates in ongoing research with the Dali Lama and Buddhist monks. They have a rich history of collaboration across their respective research areas in the neuro/behavioral sciences with and eclectic approach to emotional management research.

Their research in industrial psychology, neuropsychology, and affective psychology has added much to the knowledge about emotional management. The sidebar gives readers a brief explanation of their relationship (Goleman

2004). Goleman's and Davidson's most recent book, *Altered Traits* (2017), presents their extensive updated findings on how meditation can change our minds, brains, and bodies.

Many of the strategies in this chapter came from the people mentioned in the text box. Other examples are from written published clinical case studies on the effective use of the particular strategy.

I again remind readers that I wrote this book to be an informational source only. Please refer to chapter 8 for suggested uses for this book. This book's main purpose is to help people accomplish the first step in gaining emotional intelligence—developing a greater awareness of their emotions—and providing information on how to manage their emotions.

My years of observing and studying human behavior in many organizational settings have led me to believe that we can always become better at managing our emotions. Emotions are the key to most important behaviors in life. The forces of society are constantly changing. Individuals have many choices that involve change or not changing. These choices create opportunities for managing emotions. Unfortunately, research has shown that humans are creatures of habit who most of the time resist change (Duhigg 2012).

Emotions are at the core of why we do what we do, and they are essential to how we form habits. Our emotions affect how we see the world and interpret external stimuli. Therefore, we must continually improve our emotional management skills so our lives and society will improve.

We now turn to ways to improve our emotional management skills.

Scientific Methods for Managing Emotions

This chapter first looks at scientific methods in four areas essential to developing emotional management skills and provides information on how to develop them. These skills include:

1. understanding the habit loop and developing habitual behaviors,
2. using our EQ to manage emotions,
3. learning to use techniques from affective neurosciences, and
4. learning how to manage our environments to optimize our emotional management skills.

I also introduce spiritual methods for routinely managing emotions. The chapter ends with a discussion on how scientific and spiritual methods of managing emotions are compatible. It emphasizes the idea of optimizing the emotional management process by using both science and spirituality.

Understanding the Habit Loop

Those of us who want to improve any aspect of our lives should understand the importance of habits. In his book *The Power of Habits*, Duhigg (2012) gives us much greater awareness.

> At one point, we all consciously decided how much to eat and what to focus on when we go to the office, how often to have a drink or when to go for a jog. Then we stopped making a choice, and the behavior became automatic. It is a natural consequence of our neurology. And by understanding how it happens you can rebuild those patterns in whichever way you choose.

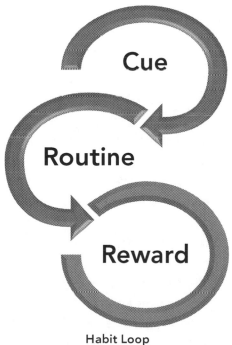

Habit Loop

This quote helps us understand that most of our actions are largely reflections of our habits; we do not spend much time thinking about what we routinely do or how we feel about certain stimuli because our brains are very efficient in their processing capabilities. Charles Duhigg refers to this as the habit loop.

> A habit loop forms when there are repeated associations among particular cues, followed by specific routines that result in a specific reward or desired outcome. The brain stores this process, and after some time it automatically elicits the routine in response to the cue in anticipation of the reward.

An example of a habit loop is getting ready for work or school in the morning.

1. Cue: alarm clock sounds.
2. Routine: Go to bathroom, brush teeth, take a shower, comb hair, eat breakfast, take medication, dress for work, drive to work, and arrive on time.
3. Reward: not being late, feeling ready for the day, and feeling in control.

When we think about the individual tasks we go through to get to work on time, we are likely to have some difficulty remembering exactly what we did. In the above example, we have cues in the routine that elicit specific behaviors. For instance, when we get in the shower, there are behaviors we automatically do without thinking. Most individuals who have developed the habit of being at work on time have perfected their morning routine so that they can do it automatically without much conscious thought.

If we examine the three-step habit loop closely, we can see how it is applicable in all routine tasks we perform. The cue is what signals the brain that some action is necessary for some desired outcome or reward. It is interesting to think of the habit loops as having rewards. We could view this somewhat differently to reflect the positive and the negative aspects of any habit loop. Many times in our lives, we behave a certain way to avoid the negative consequences of losing a particular reward.

The reward part of the habit loop is very important because this is what maintains our routines. We know from science and common sense that most people behave a certain way to achieve a desired outcome or reward or to avoid an undesirable outcome or loss of a reward. We can reframe a negative consequence so that the brain interprets avoiding it as a reward or positive consequence thereby making it much easier to develop the habit loop.

One example is the stressful job of a first year medical resident, which does not pay very much but provides a great learning opportunity. This person could reframe the reward in terms of the expected experience he or she is getting in the stressful environment and the learning he or she is receiving by being able to make and learn from mistakes; that is a reward. The reward part of the habit loop is in an individual's perception, an important point in forming habits.

> The individual's perception is a reflection of the individual's thinking's and feeling about the potential consequence of performing a certain routine.

The most interesting part of the habit loop and neuroscience is that we can form habits through mental as well as physical practice. This means that the actual cue, routine, and reward do not have to be physically present for the habit to develop. One simply needs to repeatedly mentally practice or imagine the cue being present, the routine performed, and the reward or desired outcome received and then the habit will form. We now understand that this is possible because of neuroplasticity; however, this does take dedicated mental practice over an extended period.

So emotional management is a reflection of how well we engage in habitual behaviors to maintain and use our emotions to achieve our desired outcomes. Managing our emotions is somewhat like being married to the same person for forty years. When we know another's person's daily habits and routines, needs, love language, and personality, it becomes much easier to apply our EQ skills when interacting with that person; we are aware of the reward part of the habit loop for him or her and are in a better position to practice EQ techniques to develop greater relationship skills and try some affective neurology strategies.

We are likely to discover that the best way to increase our chances of being married for forty plus years is to change some of the environmental conditions in items 1 through 3 above. For example, if you know that there are certain things your spouse has habitually complained about such as attending annual social events sponsored by work, give him or her the choice of not attending. If your spouse has excellent EQ skills and loves being in positive environments, seek out events and people he or she will feel comfortable engaging with. If your spouse has a job or is in a stressful situation, casually introduce him or her to people, books, media, or other sources that are not stressful so he or she can discover the benefits of learning to use affective neurology strategies for managing emotions such as meditation practices or mindful habit-forming practices.

Readers now have a better understanding of the habits and the importance of the habit loop. We turn our discussion to the second strategy for managing emotions, EQ skills.

Emotional Intelligence (EQ) Skills

The Goleman's (2011) EQ modified model from chapter 1 is shown on the next page. It is easily understood and very practical to use in managing emotions. The first step involves self-understanding and being aware of the things, people, and situations likely to challenge you when it comes to managing your emotions. For example, you may know that you are easily upset when you encounter someone who is very aggressive; that means you are likely to evoke a particular habit or routine when interacting with aggressive people.

The next part of the Goleman (2011) model discusses self-management. In the example presented above, self-management would involve thinking of past events in which you successfully handled aggressive people and using that knowledge to develop a new routine. If you have not yet learned to handle aggressive people, you could use the social awareness skills presented in step 3 of the EQ model to develop a new routine. That would involve listening to the individual to discover more about him or her and employing empathy skills to manage the negative emotions elicited while interacting with the person. You could use positive mirroring techniques to offset the negative nonverbal behavior the aggressive person is exhibiting. For example, if the aggressive person raised his or her voice, you could lower your voice, smile, speak in a softer tone, and use an open-body posture to appear friendlier. This would naturally flow into the last step of the EQ model, relationship management.

Emotional Intelligence Modified Model

Relationship management is obviously an ongoing process. Success in this stage depends on how well the habit loop is working or if a new routine produces the desired reward or if it helps you feel that the aggressive person is not causing you to lose control of your emotions. The habit loop and the EQ model serve as frameworks to help individuals structure their thinking about managing their emotions.

I have found that having a practical system or scheme for doing important things helps; it is part of our biology. Our memory takes over, and we function largely unconsciously when we structure our thinking by using the habit loop and rely on our emotional intelligence skills.

Experiment 1

Richard Davidson presented the experiment shown below in his book The Emotional Life of Your Brain. This experiment demonstrates the two-way communication process between the brain and the body:

1. Take a pencil and put it between your lips, hold it firmly, and notice how you feel.
2. Take the same pencil put it between your front teeth and hold it firmly, notice how you feel.

Did you feel happier in one or two?

Experiment 2

Mirror-neurons exercise to show how what you do effects what others do.

If you are a person whose behavior is calm and relaxed around others, you will notice that most others are also calm and relaxed around you. If you have someone who is very excitable, you can influence her ability to be calm through mirror neurons. However, there is also the chance that the excitable individual will influence you to become excited. We all have experienced such individuals in our lives, particularly in stressful situations. An example is in a tense golf match.

(Try this: Call your best friend on the phone and engage him in a friendly conversation. Begin to yawn silently and notice how your friend responds, even though he or she cannot see or hear you.)

Encoding a habit into our subconscious takes dedicated practice and time. Recent findings from affective neuroscience give much insight and provide evidence of how and why the habit loop and EQ are effective systems for managing our emotions. The next section discusses affective neuroscience strategies for managing emotions.

Affective Neuroscience Strategies for Managing Emotions

For the readers who might be unfamiliar with the term *affective neuroscience,* it is helpful to provide a commonsense explanation and give practical examples to help readers get the maximum benefit from this section.[7]*

To begin to understand what is involved in the affective neurosciences is to think of the combinations of those who study human emotions and the brain and its related biological systems. However, I am unsure if this adequately captures the extent of what is involved in affective neuroscience since some recent research extends beyond the body, what we typically think of as our biology, and views the mind as being separate from the brain (Chopra and Tanzi 2012).

Some researchers explore the spiritual aspects of the brain, body, mind, and soul. The cover of this book is an attempt to capture the complex nature of affective neurosciences and manage our emotions; it was inspired by my reading on how the mind, spirit, and brain respond via energy and various information sources during interactions within the self and with others. The brain communicates with the body through the nervous system. New findings indicate that this is a two-way communication process in which the body's responses also affects the brain (refer to boxed text for an example from Richard Davidson's research) and the brain affects the body. We now understand that this two-way communication extends beyond self to others through the process of mirror neurons. For example, when we are in conversation with another person, our brains connect via energy and information and we influence each other's emotion (refer to the sidebar for two experiments you can try).

The affective neurosciences are beginning to shed light on managing emotions. Clinicians use many techniques to help patients control dysfunctional emotions. One can learn much from books and case studies

---

* Affective neuroscience is the study of the neural mechanisms of emotion. This interdisciplinary field combines neuroscience with the psychological study of personality, emotion, and mood (Wikipedia).

written by clinicians. To summarize this section on affective neuroscience, I give a brief listing of some published techniques and relate them to the first two areas of the habit loop and emotional intelligence.

Practicing Clinical Emotional Control Techniques

Professional emotional control techniques that involve some form of clinical therapy include techniques the therapist and patient jointly agree will be most effective for the patient. Usually, the therapeutic model is evidence based concerning its effectiveness for the emotions the client needs help managing.

Two examples of popular therapeutic models are cognitive behavioral therapy and mindfulness therapy; these approaches help clients discover the pathology of their emotional control issues. Self-awareness is usually the beginning of this discovery. In addition, the client's past habits and environmental factors are likely to be the main contributors to issues with emotional control. With recent discoveries on how genetics is influenced by environment and vice versa, this has shed new light on how therapists can approach their patients' emotional control issues.

With increased self-awareness, a therapist is in a better position to use emotional intelligence and the patient's emotional intelligence skills to design a therapeutic treatment plan. This involves having patients develop different routines using a guided self-management plan that is jointly developed by therapist and patient.

Specific details of each of these approaches are beyond the scope of this book. If you would like a more in-depth explanation, refer to *The Mindful Therapist* and *Mind Sight* by Daniel Siegel; they provide specific details and clinical case histories on the successful use of mind sight cognitive clinical therapies. As mentioned in chapter 4, Goleman's and Davidson's *Altered Traits* (2017) gives an excellent updated and scientific review of how meditation changes your mind, brain, and body. Their research examined many of the scientific studies that attempted to assess the effectiveness across a wide range of claims about meditation and well-being. Their general findings were these.

1. Meditation offers many benefits when done with the most effective practices.
2. Meditation can lead to altered traits and brain structural changes.
3. The time spent meditating and the form of meditation are very important when assessing meditation's effectiveness.

I recommend this book to readers who desire more information on meditation, mindfulness, and clinical practices using meditation techniques.

The scientific community has scrutinized the above techniques and found them to be effective for many individuals particularly in treating PTSD, depression, and stress-related illnesses.

Managing the Environment to Optimize Emotional Management Skills

Using the environment begins with our awareness of the possible impact it has on our emotional management skills. Richard Davidson's *The Emotional Life of Your Brain* discusses how the environment affects emotional styles. He also provides strategies for reshaping specific areas of the brain relative to individual emotional styles. I present commonsense approaches based on Davidson's recommended strategies for changing the environment to enhance emotional management skills. I refer readers interested in the strategies to chapter 11 in Davidson's book *Rewired, or Neutrally Inspired Exercises to Change Your Emotional Style* (Davidson and Begley 2012).

Commonsense Approaches to Changing Your Environment to Enhance Your Emotional Management Skills

The most important step in changing your environment to enhance your emotional skills is becoming aware of the environmental cues or stimuli that are likely to trigger discomfort, which is usually personal. Self-awareness prepares one for action; however, there are exceptions. In some work environments, discomfort can be general and widespread. Self-awareness in itself does not prepare one for action; it may provide only a cue for possible action. Generally, the action can be in one of three areas: removing oneself from the environment, rearranging the environment, or reframing the discomfort.

Removing Oneself from the Environment

Removing yourself from a discomforting environment may be a desirable option in becoming better at managing your emotions. We see this most often in the broken personal and professional relationships reflected in divorce and work-related statistics on absenteeism, tardiness, and turnover.

Conversely, removing yourself from such an environment may not be desirable in that it could add more discomfort than remaining in it. We can all think of situations in which separations in personal or professional relationships resulted in greater discomfort than the situations themselves. We should consider the benefits of staying versus the losses of leaving before taking action. Our self-understanding can be limited, so advice from a qualified professional counselor or mentor can be valuable.

Rearranging the Work Environment

Rearranging the work environment usually requires serious thought and creativity. Let us first look at arrangements that do not take a lot of creativity. The first way to rearrange the work environment is to rearrange the physical workspace to facilitate communication and the work process. Everything in an office or workspace should have a unique place and be there; that helps workers maintain focus and can eliminate multitasking, which reduces efficiency. Only materials related to your tasks should be in your immediate workspace. A good reference to consult on this topic is Brian Tracy's *Eat That Frog* (2007). If it fits with your organizational culture, rearrange the office to minimize unwanted distractions or noise.

Let us look at some ways to be creative in rearranging your environment. One way is to get rid of the person causing your discomfort. If you are the boss, you can reassign, promote, or fire someone creating discomfort. If your boss is the source of the problem, there may be a chance that you and others could help him or her find a different position or lose his or her current position. Employing any of these techniques is likely to create some discomfort at least temporarily, so you must use caution and many emotional intelligence skills to make this work. I have seen the third option used by individuals who got their boss fired. I do not recommend this. A fourth option is consulting HR to seek help from an employee assistance program if available or a counselor from the organization or personnel from other trusted sources. Many churches or other nonprofits offer free counseling services.

Reframing the Discomforts in the Environment

My favorite way to deal with an uncomfortable environment is to reframe the situation. People who change their thoughts, feelings, behavior, and attitudes about a certain situation can regain a sense of control over it.

Some bosses create discomfort due to being very task oriented and lacking interpersonal skills. Those who are affected by this can reframe their thinking by considering it a great opportunity to improve their management skills and learn from their bosses' mistakes. They can also come up with creative ways of dealing with the boss and make it a game rather than thinking of it as a real threat. They can practice their empathy skills and learn to see things from the bosses' perspectives.

> Reframing discomforts in the environment is essential to master. Reframing usually causes a change in one's attitude from negative to positive.

Reframing discomforts in the environment is essential to master. Reframing usually causes a change in one's attitude from negative to positive. The consequence of this shift is significant for the individual's physical, emotional, and mental well-being. This shift also benefits the organization in many positive ways.

Spiritual Methods for Managing Emotions

In this section, I look at some findings about how spiritual and faith methods help individuals manage their emotions. Second, I look at real-life examples of how individuals have used their faith to manage their emotions while facing major life challenges. Third, I make the case that even researchers and scientists in their formulation of research hypotheses must rely on their faith to express their beliefs. Their hypotheses state what they hope for but have not yet proven, a biblical definition of faith; see Hebrews 11:1.

Researchers must rely on their faith to persist in their work until their hypotheses are proven or disproven. Finally, I discuss why a combination of scientific and spiritual methods produce much greater success in managing emotions than when using either alone.

Emotions come from our subconscious and conscious feelings and thoughts; they are not facts we can see, so the scientific method might not be the best way to handle such a fickle state. A short story will help you understand my thinking here.

When I was growing up on my sharecropper father's farm in Alabama, I would feel joy and excitement when I was with my family and cousins. We were all very happy most of the time, and we found many simple ways to entertain ourselves without TV or video games. I was not aware that we were at the extreme bottom of socioeconomic status. I was a happy child with an extremely optimistic outlook on life. I always felt that I could do anything I wanted to. Some might say that I was naïve or ignorant of my circumstances as a child in extreme poverty and that my thoughts and feelings were not rational based on my circumstances. I had six siblings each of who have very different feelings about our experiences growing up.

Some may look to scientific explanations for why I thought and felt as I did then. An important point of this story is that science can always come up with plausible explanations about why a person behaves a certain way, but no one really ever knows why one person does what he or she does. Often, people who behave certain ways will themselves be confused about why they responded as they did. This is what makes controlling one's emotions very interesting but difficult; however, this should give people hope about their futures regardless of their past or current circumstances.

> The "real truth" of the matter is that no one really ever knows why one person does what he or she does. Often the person who behaved a certain way will even be confused as to why he responded as he did.

I agree that we humans have free will to make choices about our behavior, but as mentioned earlier, the ease with which we makes choices is not the same for all of us. Genetics, environments, and the assessment of possible consequences for this or that choice influence our free will. This is why I believe spiritual methods of controlling emotions are so powerful. I believe spirituality can help individuals to persist when they find their willpower is insufficient to control their emotions.

I modified the title of this book to reflect some additional insight I gained through my research for this book and my personal reflections about my life. I added two questions for all readers to ponder: What stories do you tell yourself about why you do what you do? Why are you where you are in your life's journey? I hope these questions will inspire you to examine your innermost beliefs from scientific and spiritual perspectives.

My strong faith and spiritual beliefs combined with scientific evidence have convinced me that faith leads to hope for the future and fosters a positive outlook on life; it also helps people view their difficulties more positively and see them as being necessary and contributors to their growth. This quote by John Ortberg helped me achieve a better understanding of the role difficulties play in my life: "Suffering alone does not produce perseverance; only suffering that is endured somehow in faith" (Ortberg, 2002). Readers will better understand why my faith is stronger today than ever after they read my story in chapter 6.

Spiritual Methods for Managing Emotions

In examining works on spiritual methods for managing emotions, I begin my discussion by referencing three sources. The first is Daniel Goleman's *Destructive Emotions* (2004), which documents conversations with Buddhist scholars, Western psychologists, neuroscientists, and philosophers. One of the featured conversations is between Goleman and the Dalai Lama in 2000. Some of the most obvious results from this meeting were new insight and a renewed emphasis on research on different aspects of emotions and the brain as well as greater collaboration among researchers in various fields throughout the Eastern and Western worlds.

The second source is a more recent publication by Deepak Chopra and Rudolph Tanzi. Their book *Super Brain* (2012) approaches understanding the human brain from two unique perspectives that reflect the authors' training and experiences but ends with one common perspective. Chopra's medical training is in internal medicine and endocrinology, and he has had extensive practice in alternative medicine. His early training was at India Institute of Medical Sciences. He is an expert in the field of mind-body healing and has authored many books on the subject. His perspective leans toward alternative medicine but with a solid Western influence.

Tanzi is a neurologist and Harvard researcher who heads the Alzheimer's Genome Project. His perspective is one of traditional Western medicine influenced by nontraditional medicine. As the head of the Alzheimer's Genome Project, Dr. Tanzi codiscovered several Alzheimer's disease genes and coauthored *Decoding Darkness: The Search for the Genetic Causes of Alzheimer's Diseases* (Tanzi and Parson 2001). What makes their book exciting is that their different perspectives find commonalities on which both can agree and explore. When combined, scientific and spiritual views offer an alternative approach to managing emotions. I believe this synthesis of both perspectives is far greater than science or spirituality alone offers. Much is still unknown about the Eastern and Western perspectives alike.

The third source is *Shake Free, How to Deal with Storms, Shipwrecks, and Snakes in Your life,* by (Rodriguez, 2018). This is an excellent source for those who wish to gain greater control of their emotions in difficult times. The author skillfully uses the biblical example of the apostle Paul's life to demonstrate the importance of spirituality in our daily living.

In *Super Brain*, the authors have a chapter entitled "Super Brain Solutions: Making God Real"; they do not shy away from the subject of God's existence. Rather, they provide their perspectives on how we can personally resolve the question of God's existence. Their approach is insightful and useful since our spirituality is a personal choice.

Real-Life Examples of Spirituality in Action to Manage Emotions

In this section, I offer the lives of three people who have used their faith to manage their emotions.

Dr. Martin Luther King Jr.

Managing our emotions is a reflection of our thoughts and feelings about the situations that cause us difficulty. Dr. King is an example of someone who did a lot of thinking and had strong feelings about how best to correct injustices that had existed for many years in America—racial bias and unequal treatment of people.

As a minister, he was a man of deep faith, trust in a higher power, and belief in a divine, loving presence that binds all life. His sermon "The Man Who Was a Fool", that was published in his famous book *A Gift of Love*, illustrates this best. Readers who are interested in learning more about Dr. King will find this book to be an excellent source.

We can infer from this a great deal about King's thoughts and feelings about the interdependence of humankind. We know from the civil rights struggle in the 1960s that his thinking led to an extreme form of emotional control and the nonviolent civil rights movement in America (see chapter 14, "Pilgrimage to Nonviolence," in *A Gift of Love*).

If we tried to understand why Dr. King chose a nonviolent emotional management approach rather than a more traditional approach, we would learn that many different sources influenced his thinking and feelings. The most notable were his early childhood experiences of growing up in the segregated South, the traditional Bible, and great philosophers, writers, poets, scientists, and political leaders.

He believed strongly in people taking personal responsibility for their lives. He was an educated man who was far ahead of his time in his thinking about humanity. His life demonstrated personal sacrifice and struggle while managing personal emotions particularly those involving constant fear for the safety of the lives of many people including his family, friends, and followers.

In Dr. King's book *The Gift of Love: His Sermon*, "Antidotes for Fear" gives readers much insight into Dr King's thinking about how one can manage the emotion of fear. This Sermon is a great example of a Master Minster/ Preacher delivering his sermon in such a way as to show his audience both the science/philosophers views as well as spiritual views on managing the emotion of fear.

King grew up in the South at a time when racial segregation was the law in many states. He was unique in that he had a very strong family; his minister father, Martin Sr., set the stage for young Martin. His racially segregated environment provided a climate that heightened his awareness of the injustice people of color suffered. His childhood inspired him to search for truth and justice. His formal education and more important his involvement in the civil rights movement also shaped his life and helped him develop great humility, wisdom, and love for humankind.

I believe the greatest factor in his life was his faith and belief in God, which kept him hopeful when things seemed hopeless. His life demonstrated his unwavering faith in God and his belief that love would always triumph over hate. Faith in God's will was the only way for him to live.

Nelson Mandela

Nelson Mandela's life was much longer than Dr. King's and Gandhi's lives. His life parallels many changes in world events over nearly a century. Nevertheless, his life was similar to Dr. King's in that they both had grown up in segregated societies in which white people ruled. Mandela and King were broadly educated and had a wide range of political associations worldwide.

King and Mandela earned Nobel Peace Prizes for their contributions to the peace of their countries. Mandela's greatest achievement was becoming the first black president of South Africa.

We can learn how he managed his emotions in extreme difficulties in the many films and books about him. He had the ability to maintain his focus on making significant changes in the lives of millions of black South Africans despite his having spent twenty-seven years in prison. We can only wonder how he endured the humility of an oppressive jail environment. Indeed, he had to have tremendous skill in managing his emotions.

> "Resentment is like drinking poison and then hoping it will kill your enemies." —Nelson Mandela

In an article titled "Nelson Mandela: The Emotionally Intelligent Leader," Patricia Martin discussed how Mandela's life exhibited the main characteristics of an emotionally intelligent leader (www.http://blog. haygroup.com/nelson-mandela-the-emotionally-intelligent-leader/) She gave examples of how Mandela demonstrated leadership skills in self-awareness, social awareness, self-management, and relationship management. We can only speculate about how he developed these skills, but this book has presented evidence from science about how genetic and environmental factors through neuroplasticity and epigenetics likely facilitate emotional management skill development.

Curious readers might ask how spirituality and faith affect the process of human development through environmental factors, epigenetics, and neuroplasticity. If this is the case, I have accomplished one purpose—they are interested in learning more about the human brain and its effect on our ability to manage our emotions. Hold on and continue to read this book for more insight! For now, we return our attention to another person who had a great influence on King and Mandela—Mahatma Gandhi, "The great-souled one" (http://www.history.com/topics/mahatma-gandhi).

Mahatma Gandhi

I believe that Gandhi's life influenced King's and Mandela's lives. Just as Martin Sr. set the stage for Martin Jr., so did Gandhi's life set the stage for Mandela's and King's lives. In addition, many of the factors we discussed in chapter 4 shaped Gandhi's life. When one views Gandhi's life history, it becomes obvious that his personal philosophy of nonviolent resistance to injustice was the result of a lifelong struggle with those in power. It appears that he had a strong spiritual faith in a higher power and a passion for helping the oppressed people in India and South Africa.

Mahatma Gandhi's Practices, and Beliefs

"Anger and intolerances are the correct understanding."

"There is no such thing as "Gandhism", and I do not want to leave any sect after me, I do not claim to have originated any new principle or doctrine. I have simply tried in my own way

---

to apply the eternal truths to our daily life and problems. The opinions I have formed and the conclusions I have arrived at are not final. I may change them tomorrow. I have nothing new to teach the world. Truth and nonviolence are as old as the hills."

His passion of rooting out injustice perpetrated on the masses prompted King and Mandela to make positive changes through nonviolent means and resist the powerful legal, political, social, and economic forces in their countries. The sidebar captures Mahatma Gandhi's principles, practices, and beliefs.*

I will summarize the significance of these three exemplary individuals' abilities to manage their emotions using spiritual approaches. First, they faced undesirable conditions in their countries that had existed for many years with the support of powerful legal, political, social, and economic forces. Second, they were willing to make tremendous sacrifices for their beliefs in correcting injustices. Third, their inner strength grew from their strong belief in a higher power, which helped them maintain hope and a sense of personal control in their passion.

Fourth, their unique personality traits and genetic makeup combined with their environments' forces contributed to how each of these exemplary individuals was able to manage his emotions. Fifth, they learned and grew from their personal struggles while applying their knowledge of others' struggles. These exemplars had unique religious views, but they shared a universal belief in a power higher than themselves and a strong sense of faith. They maintained hope and took positive actions to correct injustice—they did more than just sit around and complain about how unjust their powerful governments were. They were hungry for spiritual, religious, philosophical, legal, political, social, and economic knowledge that would help them act to correct injustices.

---

* The opinions I have formed and the conclusions I have arrived at are not final. I may change them tomorrow. I have nothing new to teach the world. Truth and nonviolence are as old as the hills.

The Paradox of the So-Called Nonbelievers in Spiritual Methods to Manage Emotions

Everyone is a believer; there are no nonbelievers. I believe this because the only certain thing in life is uncertainty; to make it in this life, we must have faith that certain events will happen though there are no guarantees they will. On the highway, we have faith that all those other drivers will stay in their lanes, but we know that is not always the case. In this way, nonbelievers become believers when they get behind the wheel. Hebrews 11:1 (KJV) states, "Now faith is the substance of things hoped for, the evidence of things not seen." Drivers do not always obey traffic laws, and we know we could encounter unsafe drivers, but that does not stop us—believers and nonbelievers alike—from commuting to work; we do so on faith daily.

We cannot exist without a certain amount of faith; that has led me to believe that those who have learned to rely on their spiritual faith to help manage their emotions are much more effective at doing exactly that. Gandhi, Mandela, and King had to have faith and hope to make positive changes in their nations and in the world.

The scientific method is rooted in faith that a hypothesis will be proven correct or not and the matter will be settled. Researchers with no faith would never conduct research again. The difference between scientific research and practicing spirituality is that scientific research can produce statistically significant outcomes. Practicing spirituality effectiveness is in one's belief, faith, and hope for the desired outcomes to happen. Having hope often gives individuals a positive outlook and sets up a chain reaction that differs from that of a nonspiritual believer's experiences.

Road rage typically starts when two motorists do something that upsets one or both, but if one has a spiritual belief in grace and forgiveness, he or she is not likely to respond in a vindictive manner. If both have similar spiritual beliefs, there is a smaller chance for violence since they will have likely developed nonviolent habits prompted by their spiritual outlooks and are likely to act civilly. Their daily habits of grace and forgiveness based on their spiritual practices have affected their brains. The opposite is likely true for people who do not exercise grace and forgiveness; their brains structures tend to lead toward violence and vindictiveness. Through neurogenesis and neuroplasticity, they have a propensity to act out when they are upset.

I recommend that you review appendices A, B, C for additional help in understanding the human brain.

Part III

Self-Management

Chapter 6

Life Story: Sleeping Beauty and Me

In chapter 4, I discussed my life. In this chapter's life story, I will discuss only the last year of my life.

On November 13, 2015, my doctor informed me that I had prostate cancer. My response was denial, fear, and then acceptance. Researching and writing this book helped me cope with cancer. I prayed to God and asked others to pray for me as well that everything would work out. I talked with anyone who had gone through prostate cancer treatments. I enlisted the help of my number-one fan, my daughter, a medical doctor. After she calmed down and gained control of her emotions, she helped me review all options and insisted I get a second opinion. She told me that if two independent and equally qualified oncologists recommend the same treatment, I should pick the one I felt was most qualified. If they disagreed, I should get a third opinion.

I got the second opinion from a doctor at a major medical university. Both doctors agreed with the biopsy results, their staging of the cancer, and the recommended treatment protocol—active surveillance since my cancer was in a very early stage and because of my age. That pleased me, but I was still concerned about my long-term well-being.

I continued to pray and do more research, and I ended up in a clinical trial for patients who elected to do active surveillance. The trial uses two forms of eight-week wellness training, a form of mindfulness. Cognitive behavior therapy, physical exercise, and healthy eating habits helped patients learn how to manage their anxiety and the uncertainty of living with cancer. It is a long-term study that assesses the efficacy of active surveillance of prostate cancer patients versus prostate cancer patients who choose a form of active treatments for that slow-growing cancer. Two of the efficacy criteria are the patients' quality of life after a diagnosis of prostate cancer and the length of their lives after that.

I feel as though God winked at me with this one. I had no idea that my having prostate cancer would allow me to apply my passion for learning about the brain and using that knowledge to help others live better. I use much of what I have been writing about in this book to arrive at this conclusion. I use reframing to change my negative thinking about having cancer to positive thinking about how I could benefit from my struggles with cancer and help others who are struggling with cancer.

> The book "When God Winks at you by: Squire Rushnell is a book about how God speaks directly to you through the power of coincidence.
> My friend, The Happy Millionaire Igor Gomez that I wrote about in Chapter 4 Life Story recommended this book to me,

God winked again on August 26, 2016, when my wife, Sleeping Beauty, and I got back from a seventeen-day vacation visiting family and attending an engagement party for my number-one fan, my daughter. Sleeping Beauty and I were very excited. However, she had been complaining about abdominal pains for about two weeks, but we had been too busy having fun to pay attention to that. Finally, when she could no longer ignore the pain, we went to a medical center. The doctor took one look at her and concluded that something very serious was going on; he sent us to the ER.

Twenty-four hours and many tests later, the doctor recommended admitting her to the hospital for evaluation. On the second day in the hospital, the doctor gave us the bad news—Sleeping Beauty had stomach cancer. The oncologist would discuss her treatment options with us. Once again, we began praying and going through the grieving process. Fortunately, our minister, whom I wrote about in chapter 5's life story, was with us and helped us grapple with the bad news. Unlike my cancer, Sleeping Beauty's was much more serious. My number-one fan insisted on being with us and helping the doctors decide on Sleeping Beauty's treatment.

After getting a second opinion, Sleeping Beauty began chemo and radiation treatments. It has been approximately six months as I write this, and she is two weeks posttreatment. I will spare you the details of her difficult chemo and radiation treatments but say that we have learned to better appreciate each other and our family and friends who have supported us during this difficult period; we have a much better understanding of our faith. We grasp fully what John Ortberg (Ortberg, 2002) meant when he said, "Suffering alone does not produce perseverance, only suffering that is endured somehow in faith" produces perseverance.

Sleeping Beauty has demonstrated her faith and belief in God from the day she learned of her cancer. I have been amazed and impressed with how she endured the discomfort of her treatments. She earned the name Sleeping Beauty because she lost her hair due to the chemo, and her true beauty radiated particularly then though she slept a lot due to her treatments. She had the most upbeat attitude anyone could have during such difficult treatments. We have grown closer and have shared conversations about the most personal matters. Her struggles have prepared me for whatever might happen with my cancer.

Neither one of us knows what the future holds for our cancers. We realize our cancers could get worse and even take our lives, but we concentrate on living each day with love, belief, faith, and hope in our hearts. We trust God for his mercy and grace daily. We understand that science and medicine are God's gifts to allow us to fulfill his purpose for our lives. We pray we will always have the faith and wisdom to act as wisely as we know how while being as humble and faithful to God as we can be. Sleeping Beauty and I have two favorite passages from scripture we live by.

Scriptures

Trust in the Lord with all your heart; do not depend on your own understanding. Seek his will in all you do, and he will show you which path to take. (Proverbs 3:56 NLT)

For I can do everything through Christ, who gives me strength. (James 2:14–17)

I will return to this chapter's life story at the end of this chapter. The chapter summary will briefly discuss how the biblical scriptures and the parable have shaped our faith and helped us to have happy marriages for forty years.

Chapter 6

My Personal Faith Walk

This is my account of how I use faith to manage my emotions. In chapter 4 is a section titled "The Dominant Social Norms of the Community." I gave a brief description of myself with some clues about the environmental factors that shaped my life. Chapter 4 provided clues about my genetic markers as displayed in my temperament and emotional styles. Self-reporting on such factors is subject to personal bias as temperament and emotional style come into play, so we should always interpret these results with caution.

In chapter 8, I discuss techniques for increasing the validity and reliability of such assessment instruments. Therefore, as I give my explanation, take it in the spirit of acceptance and give me a lot of grace.* I continue the discussion in this chapter to help readers better understand who I am as a person. This will help readers make inferences about my thinking, feeling, and behaving.

The first step in any effort to change or manage emotions should begin with an honest assessment of self. I have had many different self-assessments that used a 360-degree approach, which is the best way to get a valid evaluation. Therefore, I am aware of many of my weaknesses and strengths. The most important factor is the understanding we achieve about our temperament and environmental conditioning and how they have influenced our lives. This empowers us to make better choices about managing emotions.

I have an extroverted, outgoing temperament that at times seems very

---

* As Jerry Bridges (2006, 7) notes in *The Discipline of Grace: Study Guide,* "Regardless of our performance we are always dependent on God's grace, which is His undeserving favor to those who deserve His wrath."

impulsive and outspoken. I have a lot of passion, which can make me appear aggressive. My genetic makeup of being a six-two African American can sometimes get me in trouble all by itself because of others' conditioned biases. I am relatively handsome, and my smile exposes two dimples, which help offset the tall, aggressive, African American male stereotype. But I have discovered that my presence can elicit conflict because of my personality and natural passion about certain issues and conditions. I now realize it is quite normal for humans to have these conflicts; as humans, we tend to develop preconceptions about others based on their physical appearance. When people do not behave as others expect them to, this causes what psychologist call cognitive dissonance, which can cause people to feel uneasy and can create discomfort. I believe that when this happens, people can sense that via their mirror neurons but might not admit it publicly. I have learned to cope with this by reminding myself that none of us can please everybody all the time; there will always be someone who does not like you or whom you do not like.

> You can never please all the people all the time.
>
> We all dislike the behavior of some people. Some people dislike our behavior.
>
> However, I believe you must love and respect others all of the time.
>
> When we love others as commanded in the Bible, we will also respect them. This love and respect will grow into liking. This is my challenge to all who read this book.

Nevertheless, I believe you must love and respect people all the time. As I pointed out in chapter 4, I have spent a large share of my life studying and applying scientific principles of human behavior in my personal and professional settings. I have an understanding of human behavior beyond my academic and professional understanding of it that I believe is equal to or greater than my academic and professional understanding of human behavior. That is because academic and professional pursuits are not equal to real-life struggles. To research and write about a particular problem is very valuable, but actually struggling with the problem offers a different kind of insight.

The medical model for training doctors is one of the best. Doctors must gain medical knowledge of course, but they also have to develop actual skills to provide medical care for their patients. Effectively using spirituality in our lives follows the same principle. We must have solid knowledge of spirituality's principles, but we must also practice spiritual principles such as love, grace, mercy, compassion, humility, faith, and hope to become effective in our spiritual journeys.

I was introduced to Christian spirituality at a young age in a Southern Baptist church, and my spiritual faith journey continues. My faith has helped me through many tragic events that drastically changed my life and made me who I am today. The first event was an auto accident that killed my two older brothers and three cousins on their way home from a high school football game. The second event was my tour of duty in a combat zone in Vietnam. The final event was my diagnosis of a life-changing disease when I was thirty-one.

Personal Event 1: Two Brothers Killed in a Car Accident

My older brother was my hero as well as our community's hero. He was the captain of the high school football team. The emotions I felt on the day he died, when I was ten, exist to this day. As I write this, I am crying and feeling the awful feeling I felt on that Thursday night, October 18, 1956. This is actually the first time I have openly admitted how hurt I was and still am. I still feel as if I lost a large part of my life on that tragic night. I really loved my brothers. We were all very close, and my life revolved around them. I am the youngest of five brothers, and we were extremely close as a family. I remember the tremendous emotions my parents, particularly my father, felt and how he responded to my brothers' deaths. The remaining three brothers were restricted from playing any sports, and my parents became overly protective. My brothers and I learned to be somewhat emotionally detached, and slowly over the years, we have lost the closeness we had when we were younger. I think now that my two older brothers were the glue that bonded the five of us. I feel that our bond was forever broken after my two brothers passed. It still makes me feel very sad that this happened.

This event changed my focus from being a very physical, outward individual to being someone who was inward directed, reflective, and curious about life and why this had to happen. I developed the habit of reading and sought out ways to learn new things. My high school class voted me the most studious in my class. Nevertheless, I have always had a lot of energy and felt a need for physical activity. I believe I would have been a great athlete if my parents had allowed me to participate in sports. I believe I possess the genes and the temperament needed to be a great athlete.

My beliefs about my athletic potential showed up in my two sons and their sons. One son is six-six; he played in the Big Ten conference. The other son played college football. They both earned four-year college athletic scholarships. One of my grandsons made the football team during his first year at Notre Dame, and two other grandsons are actively involved in sports at the high school and college level.

My Personal Faith in Action

You can imagine how difficult it was for me at such a young age to cope with the loss of two brothers and then extremely overprotective parents who believed they were doing what was in my best interest, but my faith helped me cope with that and love my parents. I came to understand what they were going through and how much they wanted to take care of their children. I did not blame them for how they responded to their remaining children and the ways they attempted to protect us. I believe they did what they thought was best for us.

I believe that helped me develop empathy for others who do things I might not understand or disagree with. I am always willing to assume their behavior is likely to be the result of not knowing rather than not caring. I know that attitude could be naïve, but my conditioning has made this my dominant mode of thinking. For those readers who might have assumed I gave too much credit to police officers in chapter 1's life story, you now know a little about my past conditioning.

The Second Event: My Tour of Duty in a Combat Zone

When I graduated from high school, I had no desire to go into the army. One of my high school teachers was also the school counselor. He was very pro-military and would often make predictions about world affairs. When I was in tenth grade, he predicted that most of the males in his class would be drafted and sent to Vietnam if they were not in college, so after graduating high school, I made sure I got into college immediately. I turned down an offer to go to veterinary school, which would have assured me a scholarship at Tuskegee College in Alabama, which my high school teacher had attended. I did that because I had grown up on a farm and had learned to dislike the smell of animals; I could not imagine working with them for the rest of my life.

I followed the path most African American youth who graduated from Southern high schools did with one exception. Most youth traveled to Detroit or Chicago and lived with relatives in hopes of finding a job. I moved to Detroit and lived with one of my brothers; he helped me get a job at Chrysler, where he worked. I chose the exceptional route because I knew I had to get into college. I missed doing my favorite thing—learning. So while working the second shift at Chrysler's Jefferson Automotive Assembly Plant, I enrolled as a full-time student at Lewis Business College in Detroit. I felt secure and very happy that I had avoided my high school counselor's prediction.

Yet as my high school counselor had predicted, I received the infamous letter that read: "Greetings from the President of the United States of America: You are hereby ordered to report for duty into the United States Army on January 13, 1966!"

I had always wanted to be an astronaut. In high school, I made model rockets and even mixed special chemicals as solid propellants to fuel them. I earned the reputation of a nerd, a somewhat different person. I accidentally set the high school chemistry lab on fire with one of my rocket fuel concoctions, and I caused a fire in my father's cotton field. My two younger sisters still tease me about some of the things I did in high school and remind me of my reputation of being a nerd.

The choice for me was very clear. I told my high school counselor that I had been drafted into the army and asked him if he knew anyone who could get me into the Air Force. He did, and on January 18, 1966, I was inducted into the US Air Force. I later learned from my overprotective parents that I had been declared AWOL (absent without official leave) from the army and the military police had come to their home to pick me up as a draft dodger.

I discovered later that I would never be an astronaut or a jet pilot. I also increased my length of service to four years from two. After serving two years, I earned the rank of sergeant and had the honor of being a leader. I received orders to go to Vietnam, where I was assigned to a postal unit where I supervised four other airmen; we sorted and distributed mail for the troops at Da Nang Airbase. It would have been a great job if not for the war all around me. The first day I went to Da Nang, I was given a helmet and a bulletproof vest to ride into Gun Fighter Village on the back of an eighteen-wheeler flatbed truck. That was one of the most exciting days of my life.

I got my first real scare on my first night there when I was awakened in the middle of the night, ordered to dress in combat gear, and given an M-16 rifle. We marched to the perimeter of the base where we got in what I later learned was an old French bunker, and we waited. Flares and tracer rounds illuminated a battle raging on the perimeter. I expected to see the enemy any minute; I was filled with excitement and fear.

A sergeant shouted the code word indicating that this was just a drill. I later learned that this was the routine to prepare all new troops for ground attacks on the base. That made me take seriously what could indeed happen; the enemy was very close, and I later learned just how close they were.

The biggest irony in my so-called wise decision to join the air force was that I ended up in one of the most hostile and dangerous areas of Vietnam. I spent one year at Da Nang Airbase, one of the busiest air force bases in South Vietnam because of its proximity to North Vietnam; it was a huge target for Viet Cong rocket and mortar attacks. My fears, which were well justified, intensified over that year due to what I saw and experienced.

I worked in the mail hanger on a runway, and I saw the ugly results of war daily as body bags returned from the battlefields. I was chilled by the knowledge that the young men in those bags had been just like me; they had loved ones back home. These images just intensified my daily fear of dying.

The fear of death became all too real for me on many occasions. We endured mortar and rocket attacks many times usually between one and four in the morning. The enemy would play psychological games by lobbing one or more rounds that set off the sirens and caused everyone to scramble for the bunker. Those were scary experiences; they often resulted in injuries due to everyone scrambling to get into the bunker. After the all clear was given following one attack, I was bleeding but could not figure out how I had hurt myself. I had conditioned myself to respond to the sound of the siren and get to the bunker without regard for anything or anyone; I wanted to live another day. What made this conditioning so strong was learning how many people had been killed by attacks and seeing where the mortar rounds had actually hit; some had been close to me.

Many times, the attacks would occur several times a night so that we could not get any sleep. For the first three months or so, I relied on the base siren to go off as the guards would see incoming mortar or rocket rounds. That environment honed my survival instincts. I became so aware that my sense of hearing actually sharpened; I would hear the mortar or rocket fire before the siren would go off. That allowed me a few extra seconds to get into the bunker. Others did not believe that I could get a jump on the siren that way, so I set up a tape recorder, and when I heard the first round, I would push the record button. Many times, a few seconds would pass and you heard another round coming in. Then you would hear the base siren go off.

I recently filed a claim for hearing loss associated with my military service. The hearing examiner denied my claim based on my hearing test when I entered the military compared to my hearing test on exiting the military directly from Vietnam. My exit examination showed that I could hear low-frequency sounds better after I had served in the military compared to when I had entered it. I tried to explain that my hearing had actually improved because of being so afraid of being killed. We all know how ridiculous that must have sounded to a noncombatant audiologist. What he did not understand was that incoming rocket and mortar rounds produce low-frequency sounds and that I had somehow learned to detect them. I believe it was a classic example of conditioning associated with fear or survival instincts. He just laughed at me as if to say, "Liar!"

Something else that happened in Vietnam strengthened my faith. This was the closest that I came to dying there. The enemy changed its routine from early morning attacks to attacks later in the morning. I was having breakfast with several of my friends as usual; after that, we would go to our barracks and wait for a ride to the mail terminal. On one particular morning, we decided to sit and talk for a few minutes before returning to the barracks. An enemy mortar round blew up the path I would have normally been taking to the barracks. When I got to my top-floor room in the barracks, I noticed a big hole in the ceiling over my bed, on which was lying a big fragment of the mortar round. I was very shaken and realized I had been saved by the grace of God that had caused me to take the extra few minutes to talk rather than to follow my normal daily routine.

My Personal Faith in Action

My faith in God during my time in Vietnam was not very strong; I did not think about or understand God's grace or protection. I did pray a lot in silence because prayer was not a common practice in my unit.

During a very long mortar attack, a chaplain happened to be sharing the bunker with us. I decided not to reveal details about his actual behavior, but to simply say; he acted in a way that showed his humanness rather than his holiness. Being in a shelter that could not sustain a direct hit and listening to live mortar rounds falling around the bunker was worse than being "in a pit with a lion on a snowy day" (Batterson 2006). If you are in a pit with a Lion, you could at least attempt to fight him. One cannot fight a mortar round! It was psychological warfare, and I felt I had no control over what happened to me. A mortar round hitting or missing the bunker was a matter of chance. If one hit, you would end up in a body bag. If it missed, you were safe and had another day to live. This uncertainty produced psychological or mental stress on everyone there.

Vietnam was one of the most difficult times of my life. I am currently six-two and weigh 228, but when I returned from Vietnam, I weighed 160. You might say that from an emotional and psychological viewpoint, I was lean and very mean; I was not a very nice person to be around and had many emotional issues I had to work on. However, my faith in God helped me manage life; it kept me from coping in destructive ways. My faith gave me hope and the belief that I would be safe and make it home. It helped me resist the strong temptations in Vietnam, and it helped me take steps to regain control of my emotions and readjust to not being in a combat zone.

But I did not adjust very well at first. I had to work through many emotional and medical issues. I am currently living with some of the negative effects of having been in a combat zone in addition to the physical and psychological affects I have described. My current health is affected by diseases that are associated with the exposure to Agent Orange including prostate cancer.

Third Event: Being Diagnosed with a Life-Changing Disease at Age Thirty-One

At age thirty-one, I was on track to becoming an executive in the automotive manufacturing industry. With a degree in Industrial Management and experience at two large automotive corporations, I had worked my way up to a Quality Control Manager (QCM) position. I was also pursuing an advanced degree in Industrial Psychology because I loved what I was doing and wanted to learn how to improve the ways work systems and people interacted.

Being a QCM was very exciting but stressful. The pressure of making a product that met the customers' requirements at the lowest possible cost and delivering it in a timely manner is great for QCMs. I learned from experience what stress and disease can do to a person. When one is under stress, the genetically weakest part of the body will break down or become a victim of diseases much earlier than normal. That happened to me. A greater understanding of epigenetics is essential in understanding the relationship involving the environment, stress, and disease.

One day, I was in one of the usually heated discussions at work with a production supervisor over a quality control issue. I took a break and went for an appointment with an eye doctor to get my glasses changed prior to a hunting trip. I noticed that I could not see as well out of one eye, so the doctor checked my eye pressure. He was very shocked; he said that the pressure was sixty in one eye but thirty-five in the other. He told me that less than twenty-one was normal. The specialist he referred me to informed me that I had glaucoma; that meant likely permanent vision loss and optic nerve damage. He put me on eyedrops that made my vision blurry and gave me headaches and eye pain. I could not function in my job. I saw the doctor every day trying to adjust the medicine so I could function.

The situation at work became very stressful. The company was discussing firing me. When I informed my doctor of what was going on, he became very upset. He recommended that I get immediate surgery, and he put me in the hospital. I was very reluctant to have surgery on my eyes, so I sought information about the surgery and the doctor. I found that the doctor was excellent and very caring and had lots of faith in God. He informed me that the success rate was about 60 percent for this particular type of surgery; however, if I did not get the surgery, I would likely go blind since I had already experienced some permanent nerve damage and vision loss. I gave him permission to do the surgery on one eye. It was a success, but I was off work for thirty days. He recommended that I get the second eye done immediately to protect it. I agreed, and I was off work for another thirty days. The rumor at work was that the company had changed its mind about firing me because the people there were afraid I would sue them if they fired me.

During my stays in the hospital, I had two very interesting daily visitors. One was a mortician who was obsessed with body parts and wanted a human eye. The other was a social worker who was convinced I was going blind and wanted to help me prepare for a life without vision. Our discussions caused me to think about what I could do without eyes, and I realized that therapists do not need eyes; they just need to listen to people, sense their feelings, and be empathic.

My eye doctor became very upset over the mortician's and the social worker's low expectations for his ability as a doctor and the power of God to do what appears to be impossible. I asked the doctor why I had gotten glaucoma at my early age. I wanted to blame my company and the stressful situation for that. I wanted to blame someone!

After many years of carefully reflecting on the matter and talking to experts on the treatment of glaucoma, I learned that I had likely developed glaucoma due not to work but to my high school experiments with rocket fuel that I mentioned. One day, I ignited some of the solid fuel but nothing happened. I carelessly leaned over the small rocket to examine why it did not take off, and it happened—the rocket took off and hit me just above my cornea in the white part of my eye. When my parents came home, I told them a limb on a small tree had poked my eye. My eye was swollen and red for several weeks, but I never saw a doctor about it.

I told the doctor this, and he said it had likely been a contributing factor to one eye having greater pressure in it. He said I had pigmentary glaucoma, which is common in dark-skinned people. I researched the matter myself and learned that glaucoma is associated with inflammation in the eyes. I also learned that exposure to Agent Orange can cause inflammation, swollen eyes, and skin rash around the eyes, and I had been treated for those symptoms in Vietnam. Military doctors had tested my hearing before and after I was in Vietnam, but they did not do so for my eyes. I believe that if they had, my glaucoma would have been found earlier and much of my eyesight would have been saved.

My Personal Faith in Action

When I was in the hospital for my eye operations, my doctor and I prayed that God would heal me. I am extremely thankful for having had a faith-filled doctor who had the wisdom to know who did the healing and who did the doctoring. I prayed more during this ordeal than I had during my time in a combat zone. My faith grew tremendously, and I began to understand God's grace.

I also learned something about forgiveness. When I went back to work, my company was obviously nervous about my possibly filing a lawsuit against it. They did not fire me or reduce my pay; they put me on the second shift. Nevertheless, I knew that with my vision issues, my career in quality control would be limited and perhaps short since the disease is incurable and my vision would likely continue to deteriorate. I wrote them a nice thank-you note and began my search for a different job, which I found within three months. I resigned from the company and thanked the people there for the opportunity to learn and grow from my experience there. I felt God had given me a chance to reshape my life and find a career in which I could live out my God-given purpose.

I continue to grow in faith, hope, and love for self and others. Sleeping Beauty and I are experiencing our faith increasing because of our continuing struggles with cancer. We agree that our strong faith is much more important than our academic and scientific training and professional experiences. We have learned more from our struggles than we have from our professional training and experiences.

This chapter's life story was an example of real faith in action that effectively manages emotions. The scriptures and biblical parables illustrated key spiritual principles of belief, faith, hope, and love. The soul, heart, mind, and faith shape the brain and interact with the environment and genetics to make us whole as humans. If we rely solely on science or on spirituality for wholeness as humans, we will miss the real joy of living. Reaching our greatest God-given potential and living excellent lives requires both science and spirituality. Science helps people who practice spirituality to understand how to become better caretakers for others.

Goleman and Davidson (2017) discuss some of the current research findings about compassion and empathy in taking actions to help others in need. Research suggests that how busy people think they are influences their willingness to help someone in serious distress rather than how much empathy or compassion they have. This speaks volumes to those of us who are in the helping professions. **Are we really too busy to stop and help those in serious need?**

Chapter 7

Life Story: A Real-life Wisdom View on Spirituality and Science in Healing Illnesses

Winston, an African American male in his early seventies, is a close relative I have known all my life. His mother and my mother were sisters. When I was a child, I spent time with him on the farm, and when I was a teenager living in Detroit, I would see him when I visited my two older brothers.

Winston was always the serious one who would talk about the Bible and God. I would try to avoid him because he was too serious, not fun like his other brothers and especially his older brother, whom I admired because he always drove hot and fast cars.

After I joined the Air Force, my brother Edward would always tell me about Winston. He usually had funny stories to tell about what he was doing. Edward and Winston were very close and shared many details about their lives.

Edward became very ill and went through a period of extreme suffering until his death in 2016. He and I were close, and we could talk very freely about any subject. I watched him suffer for over fifteen years going from a prosperous business owner in Detroit to being totally disabled and depending on others to take care of him. He had a quiet kind of faith and a strong belief in God, but he was not what many would call religious.

When I visited him at home, in the hospital, or in the nursing home, he always had the same upbeat attitude. He always showed concern for my family and my welfare. He was extremely sensitive and could always detect my mood and realize when I was worrying about something. He gave me some great advice—"Never let someone else occupy your head. I will give someone ten minutes of my time and after that, I forget it."

He had the ability to not worry about things including his slowly failing health. Over the years, the doctors had amputated his legs and most of his fingers. He suffered through several heart attacks and strokes. What was so amazing about Edward was that he never lost faith in God.

The last time I saw him before he went into a coma, he was extremely optimistic and talked about what he was going to do after he left the hospital. Winston would always visit Edward in the hospital and encourage him to go to church. Edward would often tell me about some of their talks and about the church he was attending with one of his sons. Winston has always been the one relative who has consistently lived his faith and been true to his strong belief in God.

Some years ago, Edward told me that Winston had prostate cancer and some complications and that he had consulted with several doctors at famous hospitals. In a dream I had about Winston, we were having a great conversation. The next morning, I called him. We talked for a long time, and I told him that my wife and I had cancer and that I was writing this book. I asked him how his faith helped him deal with cancer.

His answer did not surprise me; it confirmed everything I have written in this book about how important it was to rely on both spirituality and science for healing. He told me, "You have to rely completely on God." He said that while doctors and medical treatments were important, real healing could come only from God. He described his lifestyle and the changes in his diet, which he gave me specifics about. We discussed the importance of his family and the support they gave him. He mentioned a very interesting fact about his new lifestyle—he enjoyed his new environment and meeting and helping his neighbors.

Winston had actually changed his physical environment; he had moved from Detroit's inner city to South Carolina's rural area. That spoke volumes about his personality. Edward had talked many years earlier about Winston's ultimate plan to move to South Carolina. Winston held onto his intentions and dreams despite his life difficulties and the seemly impossible odds he faced when he suffered serious complications doing his cancer treatments. (His wife shared this information with me about his struggles.) As I mentioned previously, conscious intentions are necessary for neuroplasticity to occur. Conscious intentions are important for the medical treatment process and patients' responses to it.

The second perspective is from a spiritual point of view. Changing from an urban to a rural environment increases the likelihood of more-intimate and personal contact with neighbors. Winston is a very sociable person and has the gift of presenting biblical teaching to anyone he meets. He just naturally loves talking to people and helping them. In our short conversation, he had the time to describe an incident in which he helped strangers with personal problems just as he had helped relatives. I believe he is one who lives by the scripture, "The man answered, 'You must love the LORD your God with all your heart, all your soul, all your strength, and all your mind.' And, 'Love your neighbor as yourself'" (Luke 10:27 NLT), a very important commandment. Reading the parable of the good Samaritan in Luke 10:30–37 will help readers understand what the word *neighbor* means in a biblical perspective. There is documented evidence about the personal benefits we can derive from helping others.

My personal experience has led me to believe that the greatest joy comes from helping others. I believe that one of the keys to living a life of well-being is helping those we come in contact with to develop positive outlooks on life and find solutions to their difficulties.

Edward and Winston lived their lives striving to help others rather than being solely concerned about themselves.

Scripture

The Good Samaritan

> A Jewish man was traveling from Jerusalem down to Jericho, and he was attacked by bandits. They stripped him of his clothes, beat him up, and left him half dead beside the road.
>
> By chance a priest came along. But when he saw the man lying there, he crossed to the other side of the road and passed him by. A Temple assistant walked over and looked at him lying there, but he also passed by on the other side.
>
> Then a despised Samaritan came along, and when he

saw the man, he felt compassion for him. Going over to him, the Samaritan soothed his wounds with olive oil and wine and bandaged them. Then he put the man on his own donkey and took him to an inn, where he took care of him. The next day he handed the innkeeper two silver coins, telling him, "Take care of this man. If his bill runs higher than this, I'll pay you the next time I'm here."

"Now which of these three would you say was a neighbor to the man who was attacked by bandits?" Jesus asked. The man replied, "The one who showed him mercy." Then Jesus said, "Yes, now go and do the same." (Luke 10:30–37 NLT)

But Jesus spoke to them at once. "Don't be afraid," he said. "Take courage. I am here!" Then Peter called to him, "Lord, if it's really you, tell me to come to you, walking on the water." "Yes, come," Jesus said.

So Peter went over the side of the boat and walked on the water toward Jesus. But when he saw the strong wind and the waves, he was terrified and began to sink. "Save me, Lord!" he shouted.

Jesus immediately reached out and grabbed him. "You have so little faith," Jesus said. "Why did you doubt me?" (Matthew 14:27–31 NLT)

Chapter 7

Combining the Scientific
and Spiritual Methods

I have explored various scientific methods to help readers gain a basic understanding of how the sciences influence human behavior. I also discussed some indications of how faith influences human behavior and the roles hope and faith play in human behavior. I implied that science is factual evidence whereas faith is hope where there is no evidence.

In this section, I continue to explore the key differences between science and spirituality. I avoid using the term *religion* in that this term tends to be too narrow in focus and does not include the universal concepts of spirituality.

Most religions have doctrines that demand their followers' compliance. The terms *spirituality* and *faith* are inclusive of religious beliefs in that there is an element of hope in all types of beliefs regardless of the particular religious denomination.

The main purpose of this section is twofold: to help you examine why you believe what you believe to be the truth about science and spirituality, and to help you appreciate the potential benefits of believing in a combination of science and spirituality.

Questions to Consider

1. Are my personal beliefs my own thinking, feeling, and past actions?
2. Are my personal beliefs from my family, friends, and associates?

> 3. Have I ever questioned beliefs passed down from my family and friends/associates?
> 4. Do I feel that I am capable of making important decision without the help of someone that I respect and trust?
> 5. Now that I have answered the first four questions, am I sure that I know why I know what I believe about science and spirituality?

Why Do You Believe What You Believe?

This question will likely cause some readers discomfort, so let me apologize from the beginning. It is not my intent to cause anyone discomfort; examining one's internal motives is always a very private and personal experience that we must respect. The sciences have proven that much of what we think, feel, and do is a reflection of habits influenced by our genetics and environment, and we form habits without conscious effort.

What we believe is often unconsciously developed, but we should think about why we think, feel, and do the way we do. As was presented earlier in the book, all understanding should begin with self-awareness that includes knowing our basic internal motives. If we know what we believe and why we believe it, we will have a solid foundation we can always return to for clarity. If we do not know this, we will live very confused lives and popular trends in science and spirituality are likely to pull us in many directions.

Whether we believe in purely the sciences and not spirituality is a personal choice. The important thing is to know why we believe as we do. I offer the following questions as a start. I developed the questions based on *Super Brain* (Chopra and Tanzi 2012) and my personal insight.

1. Are my personal beliefs my own thoughts, feelings, and past actions?
2. Were my personal beliefs passed down to me from my family, friends, and associates?
3. Have I ever questioned those beliefs?
4. Do I feel capable of making important decisions without the help of someone I respect and trust?

5. After having answered the above questions, am I sure I know why I believe what I believe about science and spirituality?

Once we understand our belief system, we will be in a better position to make choices about important issues. Usually, this results in high-quality decisions and an excellent life, and it usually leads to accepting science and spirituality as essential for an excellent life.

The Potential Benefits of Believing in Science and Spirituality

The saying "Eternity is a long time for making the wrong decision about believing in God!" illustrates the seriousness of such a decision. Spiritual life after physical death is the ultimate benefit of spirituality and faith in a higher power according to many religions, but that will not be the emphasis of this section. This section will present the practical, earthly benefits of spirituality in three main areas: physical, emotional, and mental and how spirituality applied with scientific principles in these areas can be powerful.

The Benefits of Spirituality for Physical Well-Being

The most commonly known and widely accepted benefit of spirituality is the influence that a positive attitude and outlook about life in general has on the human immune system (Richards and Detter 2014). The scientific community under the heading of optimism commonly researches this. The research in the huffingtonpost.com article abstract below will help readers appreciate optimism's importance in physical well-being.

> Current theories of optimism suggest that the tendency to maintain positive expectations for the future is an adaptive psychological resource associated with improved well-being and physical health, but the majority of previous optimism research has been conducted in industrialized nations. The present study examined (a) whether optimism is universal, (b) what demographic factors predict optimism, and (c)

whether optimism is consistently associated with improved subjective well-being and perceived health worldwide. The present study used representative samples of 142 countries that together represent 95% of the world's population. The total sample of 150,048 individuals had a mean age of 38.28 ($SD = 16.85$) and approximately equal sex distribution (51.2% female). The relationships between optimism, subjective well-being, and perceived health were examined using hierarchical linear modeling. Results indicated that most individuals and most countries worldwide are optimistic and that higher levels of optimism are associated with improved subjective well-being and perceived health worldwide. The present study provides compelling evidence that optimism is a universal phenomenon and that the associations between optimism and improved psychological functioning are not limited to industrialized nations. (http://www.huffingtonpost.com/2013/05/08/optimism-health-benefits_n_3230715.html)

The Huffington Post study is one of many that consistently show the relationship between a positive outlook on life and physical well-being. The important point to understand is that spirituality and faith are often the key factors that lead to a more hopeful life, a key ingredient of optimism. However, Davidson and Begley (2012, 119) add a note of caution about a possible danger of being too optimistic.

> One reason might be that a consistently positive outlook— "I'll be fine!"—causes patients to under report symptoms, and thus not receive the care they require, or makes them fail to take prescribed drugs or undergo recommended screenings or treatments.

Despite this note of caution, Davidson and Begley provide an excellent list of research studies that consistently show the many biological and medical benefits of having a positive outlook on life, some of which are better cardiovascular health. Additional benefits are better management of stress responses, and better management of certain illnesses such as diabetes, cardiovascular disease, and asthma.

How Does Spirituality Support Science in Enhancing Physical Well-Being?

This question is answered with one word—hope. Spirituality and faith provide an attitude of hope that creates positive expectations on the part of the believer. Through their faith, believers have a positive expectation that what they desire will happen. This type of thinking has been well documented for centuries in religious writings and philosophy.

Without an attitude of hope and faith, it is easy to quit a task, but with an attitude of hope and expectation, it is much more difficult to quit. We do not need scientific research to validate this; we can simply reflect on life and compare quitters to those who persist; the latter usually have strong faith that gives them hope when difficulties occur. They are in a much stronger position to deal with difficulties than are those who have a negative, pessimistic outlook.

Having faith and employing science to enhance physical well-being will certainly increase our chances of enjoying a higher quality of life. Many examples from sports teams that have high expectations about their ability to win provide anecdotal evidence of this consistently.

However, many other factors must be present with high expectations for winning to occur. Teams with high expectations of winning are more likely to win than teams that have low expectations about their ability to win. This is also true about our well-being and general health. How many times have you observed or heard people complaining about how bad they feel when nothing serious is really wrong but they eventually end up very sick? I think their expectation influence their well-being. My thinking has been influenced by others who have studied the placebo effect and some possible explanations for why the placebo effect exist. Chopra and Tanzi (2012, p199).

"The most studied technique of mind-body healing has been the placebo effect. Placebo is Latin for "I shall please,". It's a good way of describing how the placebo effect works. A doctor offers a patient a powerful drug, with assurance that it will relieve the patient's symptoms, and the patient, as promised, gets relief. But in reality the doctor has prescribed a harmless inert sugar pill. (The effect isn't limited to drugs, which is important to remember: anything you believe in can act as a placebo.) Where did this patient's relief come from? It comes from the mind telling the body to get well. To do that, the mind must first be convinced that healing is about to occur... ... ... The big problem with the placebo effect, which is known to operate in 30 percent of cases on average... ...."

The Benefits of Spirituality in Emotional Well-Being

Emotional well-being is a subjective state related to our feelings in terms of our levels of stress, anxiety, and depression (http://en.wikipedia.org/wiki/Emotional_well-being). As one can infer from this general description, emotional well-being is very personal to each individual, which makes it difficult to develop a concrete definition of it. The behavioral responses of individuals vary for the same stimulus. Therefore, it is difficult to have a reliable measure of an individual's emotions. We know that emotions drive people to behave in certain ways. It is often difficult to discern the source of our emotions since emotions can emanate from two broad categories. First, emotions come from internally initiated unconditioned stimuli or reflective stimuli in the body.

Classic Conditioning Example

Unconditioned Stimulus: something that evokes a response without prior experience.

Unconditioned Response: response evoked by a stimulus even without prior experience.

Example: Running at a fast pace evokes an unconditioned response/reflex such as increased heart rate, pulse rate, and blood pressure.

> Conditioned stimulus: something that evokes a response after a few pairings with another stimulus that already causes that response.
>
> Conditioned response: response evoked by a stimulus only after pairing that stimulus with one that already causes the response.
>
> Example: Running at a fast pace while listening to a certain song (Thriller, by Michael Jackson) repeatedly. Stop running but playing the song Thriller will evoke a conditioned response of increased heart rate, pulse rate and increased blood pressure.
>
> The definitions are from Psychology, by Richard W. Mallott & Donald L. Whaley, Harper & Row, 1976

Second, emotions come from external conditioned and unconditioned stimuli in the environment. Examples of the two broad categories will make this point clearer.

Internal Conditioned Stimulus: Unconscious Memory of a Childhood Tragedy That Evoked the Same Fear When Paired with Certain Unconditioned Stimuli

An example of this might be reading a story that triggers an unconscious memory of an early childhood tragedy such as being in a bad car accident. The emotional response can be as strong as the day the tragedy actually happened. The tragic car accident was an unconditioned stimulus paired with a conditioned reflex—fear of death. This tragic event became part of the unconscious memory to protect the individual. Reading a story about a tragic accident evoked the unconditional response the fear of death.

Internal Unconditioned Stimulus: Unconscious Response Initiated by the Autonomic Nervous System without the Individual's Conscious Effort

An illustration of this example may include feeling afraid when hearing a very loud noise. With internally initiated responses, individuals usually have a more difficult time managing emotional responses because the responses often occur without conscious effort.

External Conditioned Stimulus: Sirens

An ambulance siren will prompt an ER staff to ready themselves for incoming disaster because they have learned to connect that sound with the arrival of someone who could be severely wounded.

I wrote about my time in Vietnam and hearing sirens go off signaling a rocket or mortar attack. When I hear a siren now, I get the same scary feeling in the bottom of my stomach that I got in Vietnam. I have learned to ignore the feeling, but when I first got home from Vietnam, a siren would start me running without my consciously thinking of where I was or what I was doing.

Spirituality Supports Science in Enhancing Emotional Well-Being

Anytime people experience uncertainty in their lives, they will likely feel fear and anxiety. The coping strategies used to deal with this uncertainty are likely rooted in people's thinking skills and spiritual orientations.

Relying solely on thinking skills to handle life's uncertainties is not sufficient to calm fear and anxiety. Rational thinking can certainly lead to decisions that will satisfy the rational part of the mind or brain, but certain events and situations do not make rational sense in many situations. For example, how do people rationalize feelings of loss when they learn of a loved one contracting a deadly disease or dying? Do they tell themselves, *This is just a chance occurrence. It's my time to experience loss*? How do they handle the naturally strong emotions that such threats or losses evoke?

If you can convince yourself that such threats or losses are just a natural part of life, you will certainly appear outwardly to be dealing quite effectively with your loss. In fact, this is what many would recommend you do. You will likely be admired by others and get approval from significant others. Then the questions become, How do you really feel when you are not in the company of others and it's just you, your mind, and inner spirit? Can you handle your inner emotions then?

> "How do you really feel when you are not in the company of others and it's just you, your mind, and inner spirit? Can you handle your inner emotions?"

I believe that during these times, a person's spirituality is at its best. In these moments, people realize that their best thinking is not sufficient for them to master the fear, depression, and anxiety life can evoke in them. This is when faith can be an effective way to achieve emotional well-being. The Serenity Prayer illustrates how to think effectively about situations in which your best thinking has failed you: "God, grant me the serenity to accept the things I cannot change, the courage to change the things I can, and wisdom to know the difference" (http://en.wikipedia.org/wiki/Serenity_Prayer).

Notice that this prayer does not dismiss science or rely totally on spirituality. It brings in science and spirituality to help individuals manage their lives. This prayer is widely used in the helping professions. This prayer acknowledges the limits of our willpower and free will. This simple prayer frees us to face the limits of self-control, and it gives additional power to approach life from a different angle free of stress, anxiety, and depression. It gives us permission to let go and seek help from a higher power. It does not take away the personal responsibility of self-change, but it takes away the constant pressure we can put on ourselves due to prior conditioning and even the teachings of behavioral science.

The Serenity Prayer also inspires us to develop a hopeful attitude that often leads to a more positive outlook. I discussed some of the benefits of having a positive outlook. We must acknowledge and accept the fact that some situations in life are beyond our best thinking and that we all face some uncertainty. We will have the capacity to handle these types of issues when we use the right people and resources. Our Creator made us unique combinations of body, mind, emotions, and spirit. When we get in touch with all four of these areas of our lives, we are in a better position to deal with life's difficulties and take advantage of the people and resources to help with them.

Some might disagree with the roles these individual parts play in us, but most agree we have those components, which differentiate us from other living beings. So why do scientists often refuse to consider the spiritual part of our humanity? Is it because they are unable to understand it? Is it because it is not popular to examine because of the tradition and belief that spirituality is the same as superstition?

Spirituality has been traditionally unpopular in the scientific community, but there are signs that that is slowly changing. More people in the sciences are examining the role of spirituality and emotional control. *Super Brain* (Chopra and Tanzi 2012) and *Destructive Emotions* (Goleman 2004) are excellent sources of ideas and suggestions for scientific approaches to examining spirituality and emotional control.

Leading researchers in this area are making real progress, and future scientists will gain an even greater understanding of how the Creator used spirituality to add to our humanity. Scientists cannot tell you why or how DNA evolved (http://evolutionfaq.com/faq/how-could-dna-have-evolved). However, they have gained much knowledge from DNA research that has practical use. Isaiah 55:8–9 (NLT) returns to my faith-based foundation for what I believe: "For my thoughts are not your thoughts, neither are your ways my ways, saith the LORD. For as the heavens are higher than the earth, so are my ways higher than your ways, and my thoughts than your thoughts." This scripture helps me remember that God's ways are superior to ours and that our understanding of God's ways is sometimes very limited or incorrect. This does not mean we will never understand God's ways; it simply means that when God desires us to understand his ways, he will give us the wisdom and knowledge to do so. History has shown that advances in the sciences come only slowly. Though many will disagree with this statement, I believe these scientific advances are in harmony with God's will. However, if you do not have faith in God, you will never be able to prove this statement as being incorrect because you will not have faith in such a thing as God's will and you will believe human intelligence is responsible for all advances.

My strongest argument for using faith and spirituality is that I believe God created science as the means by which man could use his mental abilities to exercise his God given gifts (genetics) free will to be creative and to manage his physical, emotional, mental, and spiritual well-being.

What if some day in the distant future, computers and the sciences advance to the point where humans feel so inferior that they begin to say the computers and the sciences are the ultimate force that rule the universe and ignore the real creator of the computer and the sciences, the Human with God's help?

Well, I happen to believe this is the state of affairs with man and God! God is the real Creator, not man, just as man is the real creator of computers and the sciences via God given talents.

The Benefits of Spirituality for Mental Well-Being

Mental well-being denotes the absence of any diagnosed mental illness or at least the ability to manage diagnosed mental diseases and the presence of a general positive outlook on life. Others have emphasized the importance of being able to focus mentally on life's important issues while ignoring the unimportant life issues (Covey 2005; Gladwell 2002; Loehr and Schwartz 2005). A more recent combination of both science and spirituality is the science of mindfulness. I discussed this earlier in this book (Chopra and Tanzi 2012, Siegel 2010, and (Davidson, 2017).

How Does Spirituality Support Science in Enhancing Mental Well-Being?

The above references document that the ability to focus on the important issues is the key to the most effective use of our energy to achieve goals and minimize stressors. Spirituality and faith restores hope in peoples' lives. Mindfulness is a clinical technique used to teach individuals how to focus. It takes an integrative approach to achieving mental well-being by taking advantage of spirituality and the sciences. It helps people become more aware of their thoughts and feelings and become nonjudgmental about what is happening. That helps them use their brains, minds, and spirits to control their bodies. Chopra and Tanzi (2012) reported the following benefits of using mindfulness.

- You can handle stress better.
- You free yourself from negative reactions.
- Impulse control becomes easier.
- You open a space for making better choices.
- You can take responsibility for your emotions instead of blaming others.
- You can live from a place that is more centered and calm.

You can cultivate mindfulness by meditating. When you close your eyes and go inward even for a few minutes, your brain gets a chance to reset and restore you to a balanced, unexcited state. Mindfulness recognizes the advantages of spirituality; those who have faith understand the importance of being nonjudgmental and allowing a higher power into their lives.

Why I Believe in Spirituality and Faith

My belief in spirituality and faith was a personal choice I made at a very early age. Many of my life experiences—the joys and the tragedies described earlier in this book—have strengthened my choice. I did not need someone to explain the benefits of spirituality to me because my initial decision was faith based, not evidence based. My faith is rooted in a belief in God, hope, and love. As you read Chopra's and Tanzi's (2012) explanation of how most people arrive at their decisions about belief in God, you will discover that I fit their model well.

Over time, my faith has grown much stronger by the knowledge that most of the things I hoped for actually became true or were even better than what I had hoped. When I was a teenager, I dreamed of becoming an astronaut, so I decided to do well in school and learn all I could. I knew one of the best ways of becoming an astronaut was to join the Air Force and become a fighter pilot. That did not happen, but something better did. Not becoming a fighter pilot during the Vietnam era likely saved my life. However, being in the Air Force rather than the Army also likely saved my life as I did not engage in face-to-face combat as soldiers and marines did. I have many friends and classmates who were not as fortunate and blessed as I was.

In spite of my difficult early experiences, I have been able to maintain balance in life. To conclude this chapter, I summarize how Chopra and Tanzi (2012) view spirituality as being important to living a balanced life.

Super Brain Solutions: Making God Real

How Do You Know?

You truly know something when the following things have occurred:

You did not accept other people's opinions.

You found out on your own.

You did not give up too soon. You kept exploring despite blind alleys and false starts.

You trusted that you had the determination and curiosity to find out the truth. Half-truths left you dissatisfied. What you truly know grew from the inside.

I believe that one's faith makes one know that God exists without scientific proof. "It is like the saying that when you believe that it exists, you will see it." You do not have to see it to believe that it exists.

Matthew 14:29-31 NLT

29 "Come," he said.

> Then Peter got down out of the boat, walked on the water and came toward Jesus. 30 But when he saw the wind, he was afraid and, beginning to sink, cried out, "Lord, save me!"
>
> 31 Immediately Jesus reached out his hand and caught him. "You of little faith," he said, "why did you doubt?"

You trusted the process and did not let fear or discouragement impede it.

You paid attention to your emotions. The right path feels satisfying and clear.

You went beyond logic into those areas where intuition, insight, and wisdom actually count. They became real for you.

These principles are a sort of guideline for faith.

Moving from Hope to Faith to Knowledge

The following steps are from *Super Brain* (Chopra and Tanzi 2012) help clarify the path to spirituality.

Step 1: Realize that your life is meant to progress.

Step 2: Reflect on how good it is to truly know things rather than just hoping and believing. Do not settle for less.

Step 3: Write down your dilemma. Make three lists for the things you hope are true, the things you believe are true, and the things you know are true.

Step 4: Ask yourself why you know the things you know.

Step 5: Apply what you know to those areas where you have doubts, where only hope and belief exist today.

I strongly recommend you purchase *Super Brain*, a well-written book that helps readers gain additional insight into the benefits of both science and faith. The careful reader will note that *Super Brain* goes one level beyond my views and includes a discussion of knowledge, which I believe is beyond the traditional biblical definition of faith that many religions use.

I reconcile how *Super Brain* uses the term *spirituality* with the biblical use of the word *faith* in that when our faith is strong enough, we do not need to know something exists. However, a desire to know is part of our humanity. For me, the evidence of God is his presence in my life just as wind is present in my life though I cannot see it. I can feel God's presence and experience his goodness though I cannot see him; I just know he is present.

Peter got out of the boat and walked on water until he began to doubt his ability to do that rather than trust God's power. I believe that through our faith, we can do all things when we align our faith with a higher spiritual power and used that faith to guide our actions.

Returning to the chapter's life story, we can see how Edward and Winston used science and spirituality to guide their lives. Their actions demonstrated that they trusted the medical profession for their treatments and trusted God for their mental, social, emotional, and spiritual well-being.

"The Secret to Joyful Living!"

We accept God's invitation into our lives when we believe that He died for our sins and blessed us with the Holy Spirit. We freely welcome the Holy Spirit to live in our Hearts.

1. We submit our minds to the Holy Spirit's guidance.
2. We gradually learn to listen and follow the Holy Spirit's Guidance.
3. We gradually learn to trust and obey the Holy Spirit's Guidance.
4. Once we learn to trust and obey the Holy Spirit, we experience the joy of being in God's Mercy and Grace. We are able to accept whatever occurs in our lives. We are no longer consumed by fear, worry, greed, and other worldly

foes. We are free from our best intellectual thinking. We are gifted with God's Mercy and Grace that exceed our earthly wisdom, intelligence, skills and abilities.

5. Now that we have learned to trust and obey the Holy Spirit, we understand that the Holy Spirit is our Helper and our Comforter. We acknowledge that we rely on the Holy Spirit to keep our faith and hope strong at all times. We have learned to pray and meditate continuously so that we trust and obey the Holy Spirit. We welcome the Holy Spirit to live in our hearts and our minds to guide our thinking, feeling and behaving.

The boxed text represents what their attitudes reflect about their believing, feeling, thinking, and behaving each day as reflected in their daily habits of living joyfully.

Part IV

Emotional Management and Greater Decision-Making Efficacy

Chapter 8

Life Story: Statistician W. Edwards Deming and His Advice on the Emotion of Fear

Many readers know that Dr. W. Edwards Deming helped Japan turn around its production systems after World War II from poor to excellent in terms of quality and customer service. He is also famous for his fourteen points that top management should live by to develop an excellent organizational culture. His eighth point was, "Drive out fear so that everyone may work effectively for the company."

I attended a seminar he gave for a select group of organizations whose people were being trained to implement his teaching in their organizations. My position was a business management professor and quality control consultant. I was in a partnership with another university professor and a Big Three Automotive Engineer. Our job was to work closely with Deming and develop a quality control program that my college would present to many organizations. The automotive engineer had a unique relationship with his company which gave me inside access to this seminar.

I sat next to Deming and the CEO of one of the Big Three automotive companies. I later learned why no one else had sat in my prestigious seat. It was a lunch session during which participants could ask Deming their questions. Many of the participants were from my college district. I was very familiar with many of their concerns about the Deming training materials. They were particularly confused with two points.

- Point 10: Eliminate numerical goals, posters, and slogans from the work force asking for new levels of productivity without providing methods.
- Point 11: Eliminate work standards that prescribe numerical quotas.

Someone from my college asked Deming about teachers having their pay based on their performance appraisals. Deming screamed at him, "Did you not listen to my presentation on the fourteen points?" He was so upset that he spilled his salad all over himself and went into a rage about the evils of not understanding the difference between special causes of variation in a system and common causes of variation in a system. He reminded the audience of his Red Beads Demonstration[8] to illustrate this. After this incident, no one asked any questions.

Deming was in his nineties when I met him and watched him interact with the seminar participants. I learned several lessons that day. One, do not ask an expert a question that he just spent most of his time explaining.

Two, even when you firmly believe in a certain principle and have practiced it consistently, you can still violate the principle yourself. Deming obviously understood the importance of not intimidating his seminar participants by yelling and pointing out their lack of understanding of what he had just presented, so readers can supply their own reasons why he behaved as he did.

Three, the most important point is that we can learn from this and use our emotional management skills to avoid such reactions to others.

(Readers interested in watching the Red Beads Demonstrations can go to www.redbead.com.)

Deming's teaching has been one of my most enriching sources of useful knowledge.

In God, we trust. All others must bring data —unknown

Scripture

Just as the body is dead without breath, so also faith is dead without good works. (James 2:26)

Parable of the Three Servants

Again, the Kingdom of Heaven can be illustrated by the story of a man going on a long trip. He called together his servants and entrusted his money to them while he was gone. He gave five bags of silver to one, two bags of silver to another, and one bag of silver to the last—dividing it in proportion to their abilities. He then left on his trip.

The servant who received the five bags of silver began to invest the money and earned five more. The servant with two bags of silver also went to work and earned two more. But the servant who received the one bag of silver dug a hole in the ground and hid the master's money.

After a long time their master returned from his trip and called them to give an account of how they had used his money. The servant to whom he had entrusted the five bags of silver came forward with five more and said, "Master, you gave me five bags of silver to invest, and I have earned five more."

The master was full of praise. "Well done, my good and faithful servant. You have been faithful in handling this small amount, so now I will give you many more responsibilities. Let's celebrate together!"

The servant who had received the two bags of silver came forward and said, "Master, you gave me two bags of silver to invest, and I have earned two more."

The master said, "Well done, my good and faithful servant. You have been faithful in handling this small amount, so now I will give you many more responsibilities. Let's celebrate together!"

Then the servant with the one bag of silver came and said, "Master, I knew you were a harsh man, harvesting crops you didn't plant and gathering crops you didn't cultivate. I was afraid I would lose your money, so I hid it in the earth. Look, here is your money back."

But the master replied, "You wicked and lazy servant! If you knew I harvested crops I didn't plant and gathered crops I didn't cultivate, why didn't you deposit my money in the bank? At least I could have gotten some interest on it."

Then he ordered, "Take the money from this servant, and give it to the one with the ten bags of silver. To those who use well what they are given, even more will be given, and they will have an abundance. But from those who do nothing, even what little they have will be taken away. Now throw this useless servant into outer darkness, where there will be weeping and gnashing of teeth." (Matthew 25: 14 30 NLT)

Chapter 8

Habit-Building Exercises to Enhance Your Emotional Management Skills and Enrich Your Decision-Making Skills

This chapter helps readers measure their progress toward improving their ability to manage emotions and make better life decisions.

The first stage of any type of individual change begins with self-awareness and understanding. I encourage you to use the self-assessment exercises in this chapter to increase your self-understanding and use what you learn to improve your emotional management skills to improve your decision-making skills. The four assessment exercises are:

1. assessing personal feelings and thoughts that influence emotional management
2. assessing personal relationship improvements that influence emotional management
3. assessing professional relationship improvements that influence emotional management
4. assessing leadership improvements that influence emotional management

Each method examines the individual's external and internal factors that ultimately show up as observable behaviors. Appendix D provides samples of each of the assessment exercises.

The goals of this chapter are to help readers become aware of their current skill level in managing their emotions and to provide suggestions for designing personal, self-directed emotional management learning plans for continuous growth and learning to form daily positive emotional management habits. I hope readers will grow from being good at managing their emotions to becoming great at doing so. Readers who accomplish the above two main goals will be rewarded with improved decision-making skills.

This chapter links to chapter 1, in which I discussed Goleman's model of emotional intelligence. It might be helpful for readers to refer to that chapter to refresh their memories on how to use the model in managing emotions.

Exercise 1: Assessing Personal Thoughts and Feelings

The precursor to our actions is how we think and feel; we must become aware of our feelings and thoughts that evoke certain behaviors. Bringing our thoughts and feelings to our conscious mind requires intentional effort; we can learn to do this with various types of meditation and mindfulness techniques. These teachable skills can improve with consistent practice. Exhibit ATF 1 in appendix D contains an assessment instrument for assessing our thoughts and feelings.

Awareness of Thoughts and Feelings

Awareness of our thoughts and feelings is very important as is the ability to identify the source of our thoughts and feelings and consciously act on our thoughts and feelings. This empowers us to take responsibility for our actions rather than blaming others for causing us to act.

Second, it helps us short-circuit destructive behavioral patterns that begin at the unconscious level of affective or emotional states and are reflective in nature. For example, those who learn to reflect on the type of people or situations that tend to upset them are less likely to respond in a destructive manner. I have learned to short-circuit my upsetting thoughts and feelings in various ways to not lose control of my emotions when I am dealing with disrespectful and rude people. I realize that interpreting behavior as rude or disrespectful has more to do with me and my expectations of the individual. Individuals are usually unaware of how they affect others, so I am very careful not to jump to conclusions and assign motives to others' actions. It is important to be aware of the fact that we really cannot accurately know what others are thinking because we cannot read their minds.

Please complete exercise 1, exhibit 1, "Assessing Thoughts and Feelings" in appendix D.

> It is time to "think" about your thinking- process. As was pointed out earlier in this book, thinking about thinking is a unique human quality that distinguishes humans from other species. This makes you "special" and will give you power to believe that you can do exceptional things with your life.

I hope you completed that assessment of your thoughts and feelings. It is now time to think about your thinking, a process called metacognition; as pointed out earlier, metacognition is a unique human quality that distinguishes us from other species; it makes us special and should give us the power to believe we can do wonderful things. The key to tapping into this power is developing the awareness that we have such power and learning how to use it.

Self-awareness paves the way to emotional management. It is impossible to be great at emotional management without becoming aware of our own emotions and the hot-button issues that are likely to cause us to lose it. We now look at how we can improve personal relationships.

Exercise 2. Exhibit 2: Assessing Personal Relationship Improvements

Emotional management skills directly influence the quality of our personal relationships. When our emotions get out of balance, personal relationships will get out of balance as well, and this is especially observable in close family relationships. Those who have poor emotional management skills are likely to set up behavioral patterns that set off a chain reaction of relationship issues in their families.

I discussed earlier how during relationship encounters, individuals' brains are connected via mirror neurons. I believe this is why emotional cues in relationship encounters are so important. If we are concerned about having great personal relationships in life, we should be concerned about how well we are managing emotions in those relationships.

Awareness of Personal Relationship Management Effectiveness

I believe most people do not ask themselves how they can become aware of how good they are at engaging in personal relationships with significant others. Most people do not give much thought to this matter until something negative happens in a relationship. I will examine two perspectives: that of the individual and those of the others involved in the relationship. The Awareness of Personal Relationships Management (APRMS 2) assessment in appendix D will help us understand others' perspectives.

Please take the time to complete the exercise 2 assessment and ask at least seven to ten people you are in personal relationships with to complete the assessment. Once this is completed, you will be in a better position to make choices about any changes you might need to make to improve your personal relationships. Please take the assessment, give it to others, and have them complete it before finishing this section.

Post-Assessment Discussion

Now that you have taken the assessment and have gotten others to complete it with you as the target of personal relationships, I trust that it was not too painful for you and that you gained additional insight.

Please feel free to revise the assessment by adding or deleting items that best suit your needs. In using this instrument in your personal relationship sphere, expect honest feedback that will ultimately strengthen your personal relationships. Without honesty, the assessment is of little value. It is also of little value if you do not accept the feedback and act on it, so seek people who will provide honest feedback from their perspectives to help you strengthen your relationship management skills.

Exercise 3. Exhibit 3: Professional Relationship Improvements

Professional relationships are similar to personal relationships in that awareness and emotional management are essential for having great professional relationships. Professional relationships are different from personal relationships in that the consequences of having poor professional relationships are much more severe than those of having poor personal relationships.

> Usually your family will not fire you for poor personal relationships, but your boss will fire you for poor professional relationships.

It is never acceptable to be bad in personal relationships, but my point is that your family will not likely fire you for a poor personal relationship with them but your boss could fire you for a poor professional relationship with him or her. The economic, political, social, and legal consequences are severe for individuals who have poor professional relationship skills.

Our effectiveness at work is a key indicator of our professional relationships. An organization's professional performance appraisal process meets certain legal requirements for validity and reliability that will highlight poor relationship effectiveness in terms of observable behaviors. Unfortunately, individuals often rationalize why a performance appraisal is poor and consider the process invalid and unreliable. This leads to poor acceptance of feedback about their poor professional relationships skills. When people deny or ignore professional feedback about their performance, they could face disciplinary action until they improve their performance, or they could be fired. Organizations can increase acceptance of feedback by using multi raters in the 360-degree performance appraisal process.

Awareness of Professional Relationship Skills

The best chance to get acceptance of performance feedback about relationship management effectiveness is to develop a system that helps others become aware of their relationship management skills and how their behavior influences the behavior of those they lead or depend on for their performance and organizational well-being.

(Refer to appendix D for a sample of exercise 3, Assessment of Awareness of Professional Relationship Management Skills 3 (APRMS 3). Please follow the instructions for this exercise, complete the exercise yourself, and ask at least ten people from your reference groups to complete it to provide you feedback.)

Post-Assessment Discussion

Again, you have set your ego aside and allowed others to reveal their perceptions of your professional relationship management skills, and I congratulate you for doing that. The ostrich that buries its head in the sand will not change the lion's dinner plans. Ignoring professional relationship management problems is unlikely to change a boss's decision about disciplining or firing someone.

This assessment instrument can expand your awareness of your professional relationship management skills; I recommend finding someone you trust to help you come up with a personal self-development strategy for continued growth in professional relationship skills development.

In the next section, I explore how to maximize one's emotional management skills by being a great influencer or leader of people. This is the ultimate test of your mastery of self-awareness skills, personal relationship management skills, and professional relationship management skills.

Exercise 4: Assessing Leadership Improvement

How well you manage your emotions largely determines your effectiveness in influencing or leading others to follow a desired course of action. The ultimate test of your mastery of emotional management skills is your leadership effectiveness in this regard. Effective emotional management allows you to control your thoughts and feelings and become prepared to handle situations rationally.

Those familiar with leadership research know that leadership effectiveness is the result of an individual's traits, motives, and characteristics and organizational and environmental factors (DuBrin 2010). Leadership effectiveness is one of the most widely studied areas of business management and industrial organizational psychology (Maier and Verser 1982).

> "How does someone measure the effectiveness of a performance assessment? We have found that the overriding measure is the degree to which clients will commit themselves to action and then take the actions identified by the assessment information." Harold D. Stolovitch & Erica J. Keeps, *Handbook of Human Performance Technology, 2nd Edition*, p734, The International Society for Performance Improvement (ISP).

It is difficult for those who are familiar with the vast amount of research findings on leadership effectiveness to draw simple, useful conclusions. The leadership literature consists of information from academically oriented researchers rather than practicing leaders who routinely influence individuals, teams, and organizations to achieve goals. Nevertheless, I have found one source to be particularly useful in providing simple, practical, and proven ways that an individual, a team, or an organization can measure leadership effectiveness. This source actually follow many of the recommended guidelines for measuring the effectiveness of a performance assessment. Please notice the sidebar for the referenced source.

Brady and Woodward (2013) demonstrate by example how to apply leadership theory routinely in helping individuals, teams, communities, and organizations accomplish goals. Their simple and easy-to-follow book offers proven processes for improving leadership effectiveness, and I highly recommend it.

This book opens the mind to a new and refreshing way to examine leadership effectiveness. The authors look at effective leadership as a function of three major factors: one's character, one's task orientation, and one's relationship effectiveness. The authors do not stress environmental factors as much as most leadership effectiveness research does. Their belief is that individuals have the capacity to develop their character, task orientation, and relationship management effectiveness that will allow them to adapt to any leadership environment. Accordingly, they have developed a tool for assessing a leader's effectiveness. In appendix D, I present a more in-depth explanation and examples of their leadership assessment tool. I also provide a link where readers can purchase the book that includes the detailed explanation of their leadership assessment tool. Please refer to appendix D and exercise 4, Awareness of Leadership Effectiveness Skills 4 (ALES 4).

Brady and Woodward (2013) recommend continued reassessment using the growth cycle of plan–do–check–adjust. The adjust part of the assessment requires making changes to continue the growth and leadership development process over an extended period. Many readers will recognize the similarity to the Deming's PDCA cycle (plan–do–check–act).[9] The amended step of adjust in Brady and Woodward (2013) recognizes the importance of learning from prior trials and the power of positive habit building. The adjust step fits well with current neuroscience findings about how humans grow and develop greater skills through intentional practice. This plan–do–check–adjust process reflects what happens at a micro level in that the brain and the mind to accomplish desired results. The basic facts you should know about this assessment instrument come next.

The Trilateral Leadership Ledger

The three attributes of the Trilateral Leader level are these:

1. To what extent does the leader's character elicit the desired behaviors from those he wishes to influence?
2. How effective is the leader in getting others to accomplish desired tasks?
3. To what extent is the leader's relationship with those he wishes to influence effective in accomplishing the desired tasks?

The assessment rates each of these three areas on a scale of 0 to 10, with 10 being the most effective and 1 being the least effective. To get one's effectiveness score, you simply multiply the scores for each of the areas. As an example, let's assume that an individual got a score of 7 for character, 9 for task, and 1 for relationship. His leadership effectiveness score would be $7 \times 9 \times 1 = 63$. The highest possible score is 1,000. The reader should notice that if any one area is 0, the leadership effectiveness score will also be 0. One strength of the Trilateral Leadership Ledger assessment instrument is that it highlights the importance of each area of the leaders' effectiveness; leaders who are very deficient in one area will be ineffective overall.

Leaders develop influence through five levels as explained by Brady and Woodward (2013): learning, performing, leading, developing leaders, and developing developers of leaders. Leadership development is a complex, multifaceted process. It is important to reemphasize how this model fits the neuroscience findings on how the human brain grows and develops throughout one's life. The Trilateral Leadership Ledger model teaches about the power of the unconscious part of the brain to form productive habits and emphasizes the importance of focused, intentional, and productive goal achievement to form positive and productive habits. The model also emphasizes behavioral modeling, social learning, and neuronal mirroring concepts through the mentoring and coaching processes.

Another strength of this model is its spirituality focus that becomes obvious as one progresses through the materials. One obvious indication is that the material demonstrates high expectations for all individuals who desire to achieve. The material presents a positive, hopeful view of individuals and their potential to achieve.

Post-Assessment Discussion

What was your reaction to completing this assessment? Did you gain any insight? How did your overall assessment score compare to the overall assessment scores for those who provided feedback on you as a leader?

Examine the areas where there is the greatest disagreement between your assessment and the others' assessments. These areas will offer the greatest benefit for growth since these areas represent your blind spots. You are now in a better position to work with a mentor or someone you trust to help you develop a self-directed leadership improvement plan.

The cause of low scores in any one of the three areas on the assessment are associated with poor emotional management skills. I present examples of how this could be in each of the areas.

Character is associated with emotional management in that if people are unable to manage their emotions, others will perceive them as undisciplined, impatient, and not able to follow through on promises they make. This will lead to low integrity and a perception of dishonesty. Because of poor impulse and emotional control, these individuals tend to act on their emotions rather than on rational thinking.

Task in the assessment is associated with emotional control in that if you are unable to manage your emotions and direct your focus on specific and important tasks, your ability to accomplish those tasks will be low or very poor. The lack of emotional management skills will cause poor focus when it comes to tasks, and those with poor focus are likely to be perceived as lacking perseverance and be judged as having a poor work ethic and being unreliable when it comes to getting things done.

Relationship is associated with emotional control in that if people cannot manage their emotions very well, they will likely have great difficulty influencing others who might have views different from theirs. One of the primary sources of conflict is differences of opinion, and poor emotional management skills will add fuel to that fire.

Those with poor emotional management skills are unlikely to show compassion and empathy to others and thus be unlikely to accept, approve, and appreciate others' opinions. Typically, individuals who have difficulty managing their emotions will also experience problems influencing others.

Self-Directed Learning Model

I present the self-directed learning model as a way to combine the information from this book into a systems approach for learning to manage emotions. An explanation of this model and how to use it is in *Primal Leadership* (Goleman et al. 2002). The primary components of the model are as follows:

1. My ideal self (Who do I want to be?)
2. My real self (Who am I? What are my strengths and gaps?)
3. My learning agenda (How can I build on my strengths while reducing my gaps?)

4. Practicing and experimenting with new behaviors, thoughts, and feelings to the point of mastery.
5. Developing supportive and trusting relationships that make change possible.

This model is easily adaptable to the exercises in appendix D. I recommend readers use this model as part of their individual change process to direct their continuous effort to improve their emotional management skills.

Complete the four exercises in appendix D and have others you trust and respect complete the exercise by answering the questions as they perceive they apply to you. Review the feedback from raters and compare it with your self-rating. You are now in a position to begin to work on the self-directed learning model. Use the following steps to apply the feedback to each of the five steps in the model:

Step 1: My ideal self. This is how you would see yourself if you were excellent at managing your emotions.

Step 2: My real self. This is how you and others currently rate your behaviors in managing your emotions.

Step 3: My learning agenda. This is where you will use the feedback from the assessments to develop a personal self-improvement plan. This plan emphasizes your identified strengths and how you will use them to reduce the gaps or weaknesses identified in the assessments. Your plan will require you to think creatively and act positively to build productive habits and replace or reduce the weakness the assessment identified.

Step 4: Practice using your strengths to grow your emotional management skills and reshape your neural pathways. Begin with high expectations that you will persist in face of even difficult situations.

Step 5: Develop supportive and trusting relationships with significant others from all areas of your life—personal, social, and professional. Ideally, these would be from the same group you asked to do the initial rating on the four assessments from appendix D. It is important to be creative here and seek out potential coaches or mentors.

As we enter the concluding chapters, I shift attention back to helping readers finalize their understanding of the major concepts and insights in this book. I return to a short discussion of the opening life story and a biblical parable at the end.

Deming was a firm believer of working smart and understanding how to change or manage the work environment so everyone could work smart. It is interesting to draw a comparison to the biblical parable because the careful readers will understand that one of the main purposes of the parable is to illustrate the efficient use of the servant's resources or to work smart and earn a greater return for the servant. Those familiar with the Bible will know that this parable illustrates the fruits of faithfulness.

I wrote this book to help you learn how to be smart about everything you do. The best way to help others become smart is to help them discover the power of using spirituality and science together.

I have learned to avoid the mistake Deming made—intimidating participants in his seminars. I routinely use feedback from workshop attendees to keep myself aware of how the participants perceive me. I strive to have the feedback instrument in a 360-degree format so everyone observing my presentations can give me feedback.

I emphasize the point that James 2:26 makes: "Just as the body is dead without breath, so also faith is dead without good works." Let us all emphasize faith and good works. That will allow us to properly use scientific and spiritual knowledge. We must apply the knowledge we have learned and continue to learn more daily. I believe learning equips us with the tools we need to make excellent life decisions.

> I believe
>
> Continuous learning helps to equip one with the tools that are necessary for making more excellent life decisions.

I hope you discover ways you can use the information in this book to continue your personal growth, develop, and achieve your life's purposes.

Chapter 9

Conclusions and Hope for the Future

Growing from Being Good at Managing Emotions to Becoming Excellent at Managing Emotions

This chapter will help you revisit your journey through the preceding eight chapters. I summarize the chapters by providing a brief discussion of each chapter's life story and its lessons. I also discuss how the story inspired me to reexamine and change how I managed my emotions.

When I was a young man, I wanted to change the world.

I found it was difficult to change the world, so I tried to change my nation.

When I found I could not change the nation, I began to focus on my town. I could not change the town and as an older man, I tried to change my family.

Now, as an old man, I realize the only thing I can change is myself, and suddenly I realize that if long ago I had changed myself, I could have made an impact on my family. My family and I could have made an impact on our town. Their impact could have changed the nation and I could indeed have changed the world.

Author: Unknown Monk 1100 A.D.

As a compassionate father and teacher, my thinking is similar to that of the unknown monk in the sidebar. I too realize that my best chance of influencing others is by my actions and behaviors in personal and professional relationships with them.

Each chapter's summary helps readers understand the overall framework of the book relative to effectively managing their emotions using science and spirituality alike. Readers will find it helpful to keep Goleman's model of emotional intelligence (EI) in mind by thinking of this book's chapters. Chapters 1–3 were foundational in that they provided essential information on self-awareness that relates to managing emotions effectively.

Chapters 4–5 presented essential information on social and emotional awareness factors that influence emotional management's effectiveness. Chapters 6–7 presented self-management and examples of their effective use in managing emotions with an emphasis on relationship management integrated with science and spirituality to achieve greater effectiveness in managing emotions. Chapters 8–9 offered suggestions about emotional management and greater decision-making efficacy techniques to develop positive emotional management habits and continuous learning.

Chapter 1: Introduction

Chapter 1's life story presents the case of a police shooting of an African American male. It illustrates the extreme seriousness of effectively managing emotions. The seriousness applies to the police officer and the African American male alike.

Lessons Learned

The first lesson I learned from this life story is that implicit bias exists in everyone and is biological, a condition of being human. I have gained additional insight about how complex the issue of implicit bias becomes when viewed or discussed with diverse grouping of individuals as targets of implicit bias. Some examples of diverse groups are male, female, old, young, short, tall, gay, straight, white, black, Republican, Democrat, and so on. The updated research discusses this issue and makes recommendations. I discuss the major recommendations at the end of this chapter.

Both parties in this life story were responsible for trying to prevent this shooting; implicit bias by both parties likely influenced their actions. When there is a conflict between two members of different groups, both have been conditioned or trained to perceive and react to the opposing group in certain ways based on the opposing group's negative perceived or positive perceived characteristics. As an example, police offices are trained to respond to African American males who have weapons. African American males are trained to respond to police officers who normally have weapons. This training leads to automatic habits being formed and action being taken on both sides.

In this case, the habit is to quickly take defensive measures without much time to think whether the threat is real or imagined. I think Michael was trying to protect himself from being shot by the police officer by showing him his permit to carry. The police officer likely incorrectly interpreted that as Michael's reaching for a gun. Both reacted in the way they had been trained and without much time to think. Readers who are curious about this shooting can find it on the internet. I believe most fair-minded readers will be somewhat disturbed by what they discover from their search.

The second lesson I learned is that ethnicity, economic conditions, and politics play major roles in policing in America. As an African American male, I say that this has been a major problem for African American males for a long time and appears to be getting worse.[10] The curious readers can look up the important statistics in this area. Most readers are unlikely to acknowledge the significance of politics on policing policies in America. I remind readers to look up articles on the war on drugs and incarceration of African American males.

In addition, many people feel that the current US President appears to be insensitive to the issue of police treatment of subjects in police custody (https://www.youtube.com/watch?v=ZaGQZhPt7wg). I believe that the commander in chief's attitude contributes to the issue of implicit bias that leads to explicit treatment of subjects in police custody. I also believe that when there is mutual respect and a strong sense of empathy and compassion for each other between law enforcement officials and members of society, police shootings are less likely. The impact of implicit bias training for African American males and police officers separately or in collaboration would be a great start to preventing such shootings.

I discuss implicit bias research findings in the sidebar text box along with links to two articles. Current research recommends that the term *implicit bias* should be replaced with *unintentional bias* because the former is too broad and confusing to many. The article recommended ways to improve the effectiveness of implicit bias training. One suggestion was to focus training on forming more positive and productive relationship habits when interacting with diverse groups.

> Implicit bias is the mind's way of making uncontrolled and automatic associations between two concepts very quickly. In many forms, implicit bias is a healthy human adaptation — it's among the mental tools that help you mindlessly navigate your commute each morning.
>
> HTTP://BIGTHINK.COM/21ST-CENTURY-SPIRITUALITY/IMPLICIT-BIAS-IS-NOT-RACISM
>
> HTTPS://WWW.THEATLANTIC.COM/SCIENCE/ARCHIVE/2017/05/UNCONSCIOUS-BIAS-TRAINING/525405/
>
> I believe that changing the name of "Implicit Bias" to "Unintentional Bias". is an excellent idea for two basic reasons: One, this would avoid putting negative labels on well-intentioned but uninformed individuals who have no conscious intentions to be bias to group members who might be different from them. Two, this will also likely reduce the resistance to participating in unintentional bias training efforts by all groups. However, it is very important to emphasize that well-intentioned individuals' can and are often bias to group members who are unlike them and the need to recognize the possible consequence of serious harm that exist, even if the intention is unconscious.

I believe that using the term *unintentional bias* is an excellent idea. That would avoid putting negative labels on well-intentioned but uninformed people who have no conscious bias against those different from them. It would also likely reduce the resistance to participating in unintentional bias training efforts by all groups. However, well-intentioned individuals can and are often biased against those who are unlike them and to recognize the possible consequence of serious harm that still exists even if the intention is unconscious.

Chapter 1 introduced readers to the what and the why of emotional management and provided a foundation for readers to understand the importance of managing rather than simply trying to control or restrain emotions. The chapter also gave readers an overview of why I believe this book is different from traditional books on emotional intelligence. The chapter asserted that science and spirituality are equally important in learning how to manage emotions.

Chapter 2: Jack and Polly, the Marshmallow Eaters

Chapter 2's life story is a real example from my experience of mentoring a sixth grader. It illustrated how a lack of emotional management skills negatively affects academic skills development and social skills development, and it illustrated some difficulties in formal research in understanding the lives of people in lower socioeconomic environments.

Lessons Learned

1. Teachers have a very important and difficult job.
2. Students bring to the classroom issues that are beyond the teacher's control.
3. Teachers can influence and enhance the chance of academic success and social skills development when teachers and school administrators understand and apply emotional management strategies such as social-emotional learning (SEL) in their classrooms.
4. There is a tremendous need for parent-and-school collaboration and training for children's caregivers.
5. The typical home has changed from two parents with one working to two parents who both work or single-parent homes in which that

parent works; more children are being cared for by someone other than their parents. This contributes to children engaging in behaviors that adversely affect academic performance such as too much TV or video gaming and too little sleep and less time spent on homework.

In chapter 2, I introduced the scientific foundation that supports emotional management. I presented the emotional intelligence of two fictional characters, Jack and Polly, the marshmallow eaters. The chapter exposed readers to many of the environmental factors in their family that are likely to influence emotional control at an early age.

I discussed the original Stanford marshmallow study as well as follow-up studies that tracked some of the subjects for over forty years. I presented information from recent neuroscience research on how the brain scans of subjects in the original study looked based on the subjects' ability to delay gratification.

Chapter 3: Meet Jack and Polly's Parents, Who Taught Them about Eating Marshmallows

Chapter 3's life story involved the Woodson family and their parenting style. This life story is a positive example of where habitually emotional management skills occurred daily to influence the actions of husband, wife, and three boys.

This life story has special significance to the author in that I have had the opportunity to watch this family grow over the years—from attending their wedding to watching the interactions of the parents and their kids over the years.

Lessons Learned

1. Parenting is very much like learning to ride a bicycle. In parenting effectively, one makes mistakes. This is a natural part of forming excellent parenting skills and habits. Just as one cannot learn to ride a bicycle without making a mistake or even falling, so is parenting.
2. It really helps to become a great parent when great parents parented you.

3. It is important to have great role models, mentors, and community leaders you can learn from via social modeling.

4. There must be consistency among caregivers of the children. This is particularly true between husband and wife and among the grandparents and other close relatives.

5. You are the first and the most important teacher of your children. When they act up, ask yourself first, *Where did I go wrong?* Then, ask them why they did what they did, and really listen to what they have to say. You can learn a great deal from their responses.

6. Treat each child as the unique person he or she is; accept, approve, and appreciate your children for their uniqueness. Always show empathy and compassion while being firm, and insist on conformance to your family's values and behavioral norms.

7. Demonstrate high positive expectations of each child regardless of his or her level of performance.

8. Demonstrate that you love your children and tell them that. Telling your children you love them is always in fashion and appreciated by them.

My goal in chapter 3 was to explain the parents' role in shaping emotional control in their children. I wanted to make parents aware of the science behind why it is so important to be good role models for their children.

In the chapter, I captured some of the changing dynamics in families today where either both parents work or a single parent is raising the children alone, working, and very tired when he or she gets home. Finally, I introduced the concept of mirror neurons and discussed how social mirroring works in our lives.

Chapter 4: A Visit to the Marshmallow Community—Economic and Political Forces

Chapter 4's life story of Igor, the happy millionaire, illustrates the significance of personality and effectively managing emotions. Igor is my friend and business associate. He will tell you that he once was shy and not at all considered an extrovert.

Lessons Learned

My interaction over the past five years with Igor has taught me this:

1. One's personality type is changeable at least on the surface. Surface personality changes are demonstrated through changed body language such as facial expressions, voice inflection, etc.
2. Core characteristics such as behaviors associated with implicit biases and unconscious or unconscious memory-generated behaviors cannot be readily manipulated particularly during lengthy periods of close and personal contact.
3. It can be counterproductive and sometimes interpreted as fake or manipulative to make surface changes to one's personality to get your desired results as is part of the definition of effective emotional management.
4. Imitating a successful person's personality traits to become successful can be a mistake when you violate your core values. This can lead to loss of self-esteem and personal integrity, and it can damage your personal character.
5. Using spirituality and science can keep individuals from getting overzealous in their attempts to accomplish their goals. It is always important to keep your integrity and high moral character in check.

Chapter 4 took the reader to Happyville, a fictional community where the marshmallow eater family lived. I introduced a conceptual way for readers to examine the community forces that influenced the family's emotional control. I also discussed the influence of an individual's genetic makeup and temperament or personality type on emotional control. I presented recent research findings about the link among genetics, environmental conditioning, and emotional management.

The remainder of the chapter presented the framework for five questions that examined how social, political, legal, economic, and spiritual factors interact to influence emotional management in communities and families. I helped readers gain a greater appreciation of how complex managing emotions is and understand why it's so difficult to really know the best strategies for a particular individual to manage his or her emotions.

Chapter 5: Suggested Strategies for Managing Emotions

Chapter 5's life story of the minister and the psychologist is a personal story about the author and his minister. This story illustrates how two people manage their emotions effectively with both science and spirituality.

Lessons Learned

1. Telling my life story and trying to make sense of what happened help me manage my emotions. My awareness of the life stories I repeat daily in my thoughts helps me improve the quality of my thinking.

2. Some things do not make sense as I understand the world, but I am able to live with them while continuing my quest for greater knowledge and wisdom.

3. I rely on my faith to gain the acceptance I seek.

4. I surround myself with like-minded, positive people, and I do what I can within reason to avoid negative people and situations.

5. I understand that I do not know what I do not know and that sometimes what I think I know is wrong. I understand that living requires a great deal of humility and acceptance of the fact that I am fallible.

6. I know that it is better to do something small that is helpful rather than doing nothing while hoping to do something I consider important. I now understand that taking positive steps and correcting my mistakes lead to wisdom and positive habit development and increased humility, empathy, and compassion for self and others.

7. I strive to do what I can do and ignore or not worry about what I cannot do.

8. Finally, my greatest insight in writing this chapter was the importance of how to develop positive productive habits by using both spirituality and scientific strategies in actually managing my emotions.

Between November 2017 and August 2018, I had three eye surgeries for advanced glaucoma. I was nervous about the surgeries because of the risks of losing my vision. Two of the surgeries were unsuccessful and caused undesirable side effects. The third procedure would be more complicated and more risky, and the recovery time would be longer.

My response was to put what I have written in this book into practice. I used the scientific strategies I wrote about in chapter 6, in which I described how my spouse and I responded to having cancer at the same time. I read medical articles about this type of surgery for patients who fit my medical profile. I got a second opinion and asked my daughter, a doctor, to do some research for me. Her research confirmed the conclusion I had gathered from my reading and talking to other eye specialists about this procedure. I used the spiritual approaches I wrote about.

1. I increased my habit of praying to God daily and asking others to pray that God would give my doctor the skills and the wisdom to know how best to perform this surgical procedure.
2. I asked the doctor, "If your parents had the same medical problems as I do, would you recommend the same treatment for them?" I then watched their body language to see if it matched what they said.
3. I expressed confidence in the doctor's skills and my faith that the procedure would go well.
4. I started using mindfulness and stress-management techniques and meditated to build resilience. I am experimenting with making my meditation techniques compatible with my Christian beliefs.

My main goal in writing chapter 5 was to share important information about how readers could use both spiritual and scientific strategies to manage emotions. I wanted to help readers discover from a self-directed learning approach how they could effectively manage emotions and continue to grow their emotional management skills.

Chapter 5 presented two broad categories of strategies for managing emotions. The first included many scientifically proven and tested techniques from clinical and research perspectives. I chose an eclectic approach to get a very broad-based survey from the most relevant areas. The latest emotional management techniques have emerged from more in-depth understanding in psychology, business, neurology, genetics, and other new areas such as affective neuroscience and epigenetics.

The second category included spiritual methods for managing emotions. An individual's belief system may or may not rely on scientific methods, but this chapter presented samples of scientific research studies that support the use of spiritual methods.

Chapter 5 also presented examples of what I referred to as the three champions of emotional management: Dr. Martin Luther King Jr., Nelson Mandela, and Mahatma Gandhi. Their great emotional management skills changed the lives of billions of people and the entire world. Their secrets to achieving such great skills in emotional management lie in a simple but proven method for developing great emotional management skills.

The unknown monk of AD 1100 best illustrates this secret. His famous poem is at the beginning of this chapter in a sidebar. Gandhi's, King's, and Mandela's behaviors demonstrated the unknown monk's poem in action to change the world first by controlling themselves. Their daily habits of effectively managing their emotions ultimately shaped their lives and helped them become worldwide icons of peace and justice. They have set examples of how to use spirituality to manage emotions.

An additional source, I discussed in chapter 5 the work of Herbert Benson, famous for his work in stress management and the use of the relaxation response (Benson and Klipper 2000). He also is a very strong believer in the power of faith and in what he referred to as *self-care,* describing spiritual approaches as one leg of a three-legged stool model inclusive of medical practice (i.e., drugs, surgeries, and self-care). Readers who wish to learn about recent works in this area can consult this link: http://bensonhenryinstitute.org/index.php/news-and-events/bhi-news.

Chapter 6: My Personal Faith Walk

Chapter 6's life story, Sleeping Beauty and Me, reflected my wife's and my current struggles with cancer. I asked myself, *Why would God allow both my wife and me to have cancer at the same time?* After much reflection, I asked myself, *What is so special about my wife and me that we would be exempt from having cancer at the same time?*

Lessons Learned

1. I began my preparation for such a condition some four years ago by researching and writing this book. At least I was able to make some sense of this and accept the fact that we both had cancer. I feel like I am prepared to handle whatever happens.
2. This gave me the unwanted opportunity to put my faith in action. We began to pray more and asked everyone we knew to pray for us.
3. We learned to rely on science for our treatments. We are in consultation with oncologists from major research hospitals that specialize in treating our types of cancer.
4. We have rediscovered the joy of having each other as friends and spouses.
5. I rediscovered my wife's true beauty. She became even more beautiful after she lost her hair due to the chemo and radiation treatments; she was sleeping a lot at that time, so I started calling her Sleeping Beauty.
6. We have gained a greater appreciation of each other and the many gifts of life.
7. We are on a journey of continuous growth and learning in effectively managing our emotions associated with living with cancer.
8. We have concluded that helping and serving others is the true purpose for our lives. This is not a new discovery for us. Sleeping Beauty has spent most of her professional life as a special-education teacher, principal, college administrator, and community volunteer.
9. We see this as a renewed opportunity to continue helping others with their struggles of effectively managing their emotions.
10. Life is truly a process of practicing positive daily habits and practicing replacing, reducing, or eliminating negative habits.

In chapter 6, I presented examples of three life-changing events. One of the events was the year I spent in Vietnam in a combat zone. I presented the events to help readers understand how my faith has continued to grow and develop.

Chapter 7: The Combination of the Scientific Method and Spiritual Methods Produces a Greater Benefit

Chapter 7's life story dealt with Winston's and Edward's wisdom about spirituality and science in healing illnesses. Their story showed how long-term relationships are essential to the optimal use of science and spirituality in effective emotional management.

Lessons Learned

I observed my brother, Edward, over his life and specifically the last fifteen years as he struggled with illnesses that took his life in 2016. Winston endured by relying on his faith in God. I asked him, "How do you use your faith in God?" He said, "In everything, God is the one who does the healing." I have learned this:

1. Personal and close relationships with many diverse individuals add meaning to and prolong life.
2. Forgiveness frees us from feelings of guilt and vengeance so we can deal with important life issues.
3. Maintaining a positive attitude regardless of one's conditions helps a serious illness appear manageable and enables one to live a higher quality life with greater acceptance and well-being.
4. Having a dream or something that you are passionate about is very important and adds meaning to life.
5. Being concerned about others more than self is therapeutic and helps with your issues and illnesses.
6. I saw that Edward and Winston tried to live by Luke 10:27 (NLT): "The man answered, 'You must love the LORD your God with all your heart, all your soul, all your strength, and all your mind.' And, 'Love your neighbor as yourself.'"
7. Edward and Winston were excellent role models for how to use spirituality and science in effectively managing emotions. They developed and maintained life-long relationships.

Chapter 7 opened with a discussion of why we believe as we do and discussed the potential benefits of believing in spirituality and science. I discussed why I believed in spirituality and faith.

I ended the chapter with a discussion from the book *The Super Brain* and gave the authors' views on moving from hope to faith and knowledge. Additionally, I made the point that my views differed from those of the authors of *The Super Brain* on the importance of knowledge in spirituality. My view was that faith in God was not a matter of knowledge but of belief, hope, and trust in God's existence.

Chapter 8: Suggested Habit Skill-Building Exercises to Enhance your Emotional Management Skills and Enrich Your Decision Making

Chapter 8's life story was of W. Edwards Deming and his advice on the emotion of fear. I presented his story to emphasize two main points. First, our personal perceptions of how we behave are often inaccurate; that means we need feedback from others who are in positions to objectively observe us and give unbiased feedback.

Second, one of the best ways to improve behavior is to measure it and give feedback that is perceived as reinforcement. That will help change undesirable behaviors to desirable behaviors. Deming and others developed self-generating feedback systems using statistical control techniques for organizations to accomplish these two points.

Lessons Learned

1. Everyone can benefit from objective feedback about their ability to manage their emotions.
2. We all have blind spots when judging our personal skill levels.
3. Learning occurs via practicing the correct habits that leads to desired skills.
4. We must realize we will make mistakes in the habit-building process, and we must spend time and effort to develop the necessary skills. This is a natural path in the process of becoming excellent at managing personal emotions.

5. We must take desirable actions (behaving, thinking, and feeling) to accomplish a desired task. If we succeed, we are likely to make that a habit.
6. We must avoid undesirable actions such as procrastinating.
7. We must develop or already have very strong reasons for improving our emotional management skills.

In reviewing the lessons learned in chapters 3–5, we see how neuroscience plays a role in changing the brain throughout our lives. Deming viewed an organization as a system with many processes that produced outputs. He viewed each process as having two major sources of variation that influenced the quality of its output—the common-cause variation in which the process was stable and functioning as expected, and the special-cause variation in which the process was not performing as expected.

Deming recommended that organizations use statistical techniques based on actual feedback data from the process to determine if the process was or was not in control. Similarly, scientists, clinicians, therapists, and medical professionals use neuroscience and other human science techniques while understanding that the human body functions as a system with many processes that influence the quality of those processes. Clinicians can use feedback data from their clients or patients to suggest actions they can take to correct out-of-control behaviors that contributes to or causes dysfunction.

Chapter 8 presented four habit skill-building exercises in the multi-rater format that requires self-rating and the ratings from individuals who know you well. This improves the validity and reliability of the skill-building exercise. The chapter gives a brief description of the skill-building exercise and instructions on how to administer them. Each skill-building exercise has a section for post-assessment discussion.

I ended the chapter by presenting the self-directed learning model from *Primal Leadership* (Goleman et al. 2002). The self-directed model offers a systematic way of integrating an individual's self-development efforts to increase the chances of achieving maximum self-effectiveness.

Suggestions for Using This Book

I hope this book inspires readers to learn more about how spirituality and science interact in our lives. My life's passion has evolved from a childhood love of learning to an adult search for ways to enrich human existence. I believe that God holds the key to our enriched existence and that science is a vehicle God has given us. I believe we all have the innate capacity to tap into spirituality and develop the wisdom to use science to enrich rather than destroy humanity. I hope you share my opinion on the importance of using spirituality and science together.

I recommend that you use this book as a reference guide to more scientifically oriented books that provide a more in-depth explanation of the human brain and mind. I recommend that this book be used as part of an educational curriculum in which objectivity and inclusiveness are valued as important assets to learners. I believe this will be an important resource for an individual or a group that desires to learn how science and spirituality together can allow people to effectively manage their emotions more so than using either alone can.

References

Allami, N., Y. Paulignan, A. Brovelli, and D. Boussaoud. (2008). "Visuo-motor learning with combination of different rates of motor imagery and physical practice." *Experimental Brain Research* 184(1): 105–13.

Batterson, M. (2006). *In a pit with a lion on a snowy day.* Nashville, TN: Multnomah.

Benson, H., and M. Z. Klipper. (2000). *The relaxation response.* New York: HarperCollins.

Bridges, J. (2006). *The discipline of grace: Study guide.* Colorado Springs, CO: NavPress.

Brady, C., and O. Woodward. (2013). *Financial fitness: The offense, defense, and playing field of personal finance.* Flint, MI: Obstacles Press.

Casey, B. J., L. H. Somerville, H. Gotlib, O. Ayduk, N. Franklin, M. K. Askren, J. Jonides, M. G. Berman, N. L. Wilon, T, Teslovich, G. Glover, V. Zayas, W. Mischel, and Y. Shoda. (2011). "Behavioral and neural correlates of delay of gratification 40 years later." *Proceedings of the National Academy of Sciences* 108(36): 14988–15003.

Chopra, D., and R. E. Tanzi. (2012). *Super brain: Unleashing the explosive power of your mind to maximize health, happiness, and spiritual well-being.* New York: Harmony Book.

Chilton, S., M. Rukstalis, and A. K. Gregory. (2016). *The Rewired Brain: Free yourself of Negative Behavior and Release Your Best Self.* Grand Rapid, MI: BakerBooks.

Cisek, P., and J. F. Kalaska. (2004). "Neural correlates of mental rehearsal in dorsal premotor cortex." *Nature* 431: 993–96.

Costa, P. T. Jr. and R. R. McCrae. (1992). *Revised NEO Personality Inventory (NEO-PI-R) and NEO Five-Factor Inventory (NEO-FFI) manual.* Odessa, FL: Psychological Assessment Resources.

Covey, S. R. (2005). *The 8ᵗʰ habit from effectiveness to greatness.* New York: Free Press.

Davidson, R. J., and S. Begley. (2012). *The emotional life of your brain: How its unique patterns affect the way you think, feel, and live and how you can change them.* New York: Hudson Street Press.

DuBrin, A. J. (2010). *Leadership: Research findings, practices, and skills* (4ᵗʰ ed.). Mason, OH: Cengage Learning.

Duhigg, C. (2012). *The power of habit.* New York: Random House.

Eamon, M. K. (2001). "The effects of poverty on children's socioemotional development: An ecological systems analysis." *Social Work* 46(3): 256–66.

Ferster, C. B., and B. F. Skinner. (1957). *Schedules of reinforcement.* East Norwalk, CT: Appleton-Century-Crofts.

Gilbert, D. (1998). *The American class structure.* New York: Wadsworth.

Gladwell, M. (2002). *The tipping point.* New York: Little, Brown.

Goleman, D. (1986). *Vital lies, simple truth: The psychology of self-deception.* New York: Simon and Schuster.

Goleman, D. (2004). *Destructive emotions: A scientific dialogue with the Dalai Lama.* New York: Bantam Dell.

Goleman, D. (2011). *The brain and emotional intelligence: New insights.* Northampton, MA: More Than Sound.

Goleman, D., R. Boyatziz, and A. Mckee. (2002). *Primal leadership: Realizing the power of emotional intelligence.* Boston: Harvard Business School Press.

Kelly, M., W. McGowen, and C. Williams. (2014). *BUSN6, Introduction to business.* Independence, KY: Cengage Learning.

King, M. L. K. Jr. (2012). *A gift of love; Sermons from Strength to Love and other preachings.* Boston: Beacon Press.

Littauer, F. (1992). *Personality plus: How to understand others by understanding yourself.* Grand Rapids, MI: Flemming H. Revell.

Loehr, J., and T. Schwartz. (2005). *The power of full engagement.* New York: Free Press.

Maier, N. R. F., and G. C. Verser. (1982). *Psychology in industrial organization.* Boston: Houghton Mifflin.

Mischel, W., E. B. Ebbesen, and A. Zeiss (1972). "Cognitive and attentional mechanisms in delay of gratification." *Journal of Personality and Social Psychology* 21(2): 204–18.

Oakley, B. (2007). *Evil genes: Why Rome fell, Hitler rose, Enron failed, and my sister stole my mother's boyfriend.* Amherst, NY: Prometheus Books.

Richards, S. and A. Detter. (2014). "Cancer immunotherapy's untapped potential inspires optimism"; http://www.fhcrc.org/en/news/center-news/2014/04/whats-hot-in-cancer-immunotherapy.html.

Rothbart, M. K., S. A. Ahadi, and D. Evans. (2000). "Temperament and personality: Origins and outcomes." *Journal of Personality and Social Psychology* 78(1): 122-1135.

Saß, H. (2001). "Personality disorders." In N. J. Smelser and P. B. Baltes, eds., *International encyclopedia of the social and behavioral sciences* (11301–308). Amsterdam: Elsevier.

Siegel, D. J. (2010). *The mindful therapist.* New York: W.W. Norton.

Shoda, Y., W. Mischel, and P. K. Peake. (1990). "Predicting adolescent cognitive and self-regulatory competencies from preschool delay of gratification: Identifying diagnostic conditions." *Developmental Psychology* 26(6): 978–86.

Steingold, F. S. (2003). *The employer's legal handbook,* fifth ed. Berkley, CA: NOLO Press.

Tanzi, R. E., and A. B. Parson. (2001). *Decoding darkness: The search for the genetic causes of Alzheimer's diseases.* Cambridge, MA: Perseus.

Tracy, B. (2007). *Eat that frog.* San Francisco: Berrett-Koehler.

Von Hippel, W., and R. Trivers. (2011). "The evolution and psychology of self-deception." *Behavioral and Brain Sciences* 34(1): 1–16.

Waitley, D. (1986). *The psychology of winning.* New York: Berkley.

Part V

Appendices

Easily Understood Definitions Using the Author's Explanations

Human Brain (Namuh Niarb): used in this book to explain the functions of the three main areas of the brain.

Triune Brain: the three major structures of the human brain.

1. The brain stem: most commonly associated with major life-supporting activities such as controlling the autonomic nervous system. It is in the back bottom part of the human brain on the top of the spinal cord.

2. The limbic area: most commonly associated with emotional responses and survival instincts. Sometimes referred to as the reptilian part of the human brain. It is in the deep, middle back part of the brain.

3. The cerebral cortex: most commonly referred to as the right or left hemisphere of the brain. Most commonly associated with unique human qualities such as memory, perception, thinking, or other higher-order human functions. It is in the top part of the human skull extending to the sides of the head.

    a. **high-road functions:** Namuh Niarb travels this road when she demonstrates by her actions that her performance is at peak levels. She is managing her emotions very effectively. This has resulted in excellent decision making and a life that demonstrates well-being (the cerebral cortex).

    b. **low-road functions:** Namuh Niarb travels this road when he is unable to control his emotions, unable to think clearly, handles stressful situations poorly, and is prone to making poor decisions or procrastinating and failing to take important actions. This is being emotionally hijacked and traveling the low road (the limbic area and the brain stem).

Epigenetics: the process by which genes are expressed, turned on, or turned off.

Metacognition: the ability to think about thinking.

Neuroplasticity: the process by which the human brain changes and grows new connections. This process begins at birth and continues until death (technically, the process begins before birth).

Mind-Spirit-Soul (Dnim Tirips Luos): the seeds of humanity. The part of human beings that makes them uniquely different from other life forms. The part of human beings that is most misunderstood and I believe the most important in determining how we ultimately manage our emotions.(This is the author's definition).

Neurogenesis: The process that underlies neuroplasticity in which the growth of new stem cells splits and forms new neurons that facilitate neuroplasticity.

Appendix B

Human Brain (Spelled Backward Namuh Niarb)

Namuh Niarb (*human brain spelled backward. Note to readers. The following story describes how each individual brain typically functions. I used the stereo-typing view of how people characterize the different hemispheres of the human brain. The Right brain is usually thought of as the emotional side and the Left side is thought of as the rational or logical side. A more accurate characterization of the brain hemispheres function is that males and females used both sides of their brains and it is difficult to know how exactly they use their brains in a given situation.*)

Namuh Niarb is an eccentric one from India. Except for a very few select intellectuals, most people misunderstand him. Most individuals describe Namuh Niarb by what he does at important milestones of his physical development; however, describing him in this way gives one only an academic or logical understanding of him.

It is easy to miss many aspects of Namuh Niarb because they are not obvious, and many fail to understand why he behaves as he does. He tends to focus attention on things he likes or fears. This is how neuroplasticity begins. A simple way to understand this is with a quote from the Bible, "For as he thinketh in his heart, so is he" (Proverbs 23:7 KJV). Whatever we put concentrated, intentional effort into over an extended period will grow in strength. This is also true of the components of Namuh Niarb, and it is the key to understanding his behavioral development.

Namuh has an unusual appetite—he likes the same things the human heart likes. If you were his parents, you would find it easy to keep him physically healthy simply by giving him heart-healthy food. If you wanted to keep him spiritually healthy, you would need to feed him spiritually inspiring information.

He really is a social fellow. A special part of his personality that allows him to be social is his sister, Right Brain. She generally helps him to be more social than he would be on his own. She is also much more sensitive to the environment and others. On the other hand, Left Brain tends to make him less social and more insensitive to his environment.

Both have this very unusual ability to transmit their feelings to others close by without speaking; they telepathically emit a signal that causes others to react in their presence. I have observed Namuh Niarb walking into a room with a big smile on his face that prompts others to smile. Right Brain does a similar thing with her boss and spouse. She can finish their sentences during a conversation with amazing accuracy. It is almost as if she can read their minds. When she comes into the office in the morning, the entire office environment changes to reflect her mood.

One morning, Right Brain had an argument with her husband before she left for work. When she got there, her outward appearance was normal, but she projected very strong feelings into the office environment. Her supervisor, Jim, noticed these feelings and somehow telepathically sent the negative feelings throughout the entire office. Just like Right Brain, her Left Brain, Supervisor, Jim, had an equally powerful ability to transmit feelings throughout an environment without a word. We all do. However, Left Brain is usually unaware of how others are likely to respond to his feelings. Right Brain is usually aware of how people are likely to respond to her feelings, and she uses that to her advantage in the environment to manage emotions. This process is reciprocal and happens between individuals. In fact, our ability to manage our emotions and influence others' emotions is one of Namuh's dominant features and is the core of leadership competence.

I have gotten to know Namuh and watched what makes him tick. I have observed three major influences on him that I call the Triune Niarb factors (Triune Brain). If you are familiar with the Bible and understand the biblical concept of the Triune God, you will find that Namuh Niarb functions in a similar manner.

Triune (brain)Niarb Factors

The first of the Triune Niarb factors I refer to as survival factors (the brain stem). This is Namuh's ability to do what it takes to get what he desires or avoid what he dislikes. This gives him the qualities that sustain life's major functions.

I refer to the second set of factors as the mediating factors (the cortex areas) that keep Namuh in touch with reality; they help him understand how others are likely to see him and respond to him. They also help him think about how he is thinking.

The third set of factors, the higher-order factors (the limbic area), separates humans from other species. These factors are associated with things such as moral judgments, time, and a sense of self. Whenever I am confused about why Namuh is acting a certain way, it helps me to understand how the Triune Niarb factors might be influencing his behavior.

A much easier way to understand Namuh Niarb is to understand the road he is on any one day. If he is on the high road, he is managing his emotions effectively and making excellent decisions. If he is on the low road, he is doing a poor job of controlling his emotions, can make poor decisions, and feel stressed and unhappy.

How Triune (brain) Niarb Factors Influence (human's) Namuh's Behavior

In certain situations, Namuh acts like a very nice individual, but in other situations, he is an out of control and angry individual. Most of the time, however, Namuh is not at either extreme and gets along well with most people. I have discovered why he acts as he does in different situations.

The Very Nice Namuh Niarb

It was a nice warm spring day in April 2008. Namuh awakened from a very restful eight hours of sleep. He had a nutritional and heart-healthy breakfast and was anticipating his friends' arrival. He thought about how the day was likely to go, and he became more excited because he recalled how he and his friends would have great days together. He visualized how he would feel and what his friends would say to him. A car horn pleasantly interrupted his thoughts. He leaped to his feet and rushed out to meet his friends.

Analysis of the Nice or Calm Triune Niarb Factors

An analysis of the Triune Niarb factors will help readers understand why Namuh acted like a very nice person that day. First, his survival factors were all very favorable. He faced no real or imagined threats, and his bodily functions were at their peak. He had received adequate nourishment, rest, and sleep.

Second, his mediating factors helped create a sense of control over the situation and his life. He was in a joyful state. He thought about the last time he had felt that way and how it had turned out to be just as he had thought.

Finally, Triune Niarb's high-order factors kicked in and brought him back to reality about what time it was and what was happening when he heard the car horn. These factors helped him be in the present with his friends and make personal value judgments about each one. He greeted them warmly with high-fives and hugged his two female friends. He noticed his friends were all very happy as they greeted him. He noticed the very expensive jewelry one of his friends was wearing; that made him feel at ease for wearing his Rolex watch.

The Very Nasty Triune Namuh Niarb

Triune Niarb returned from vacation with his friends a week later on another nice warm April day. He had not slept well the previous night. He was feeling tired. He did not feel like eating. A virus he had picked up on vacation made him unable to sleep or eat. He recounted events that upset him while he was on vacation with his friends. There were issues about sharing the expenses, and he ended up spending twice as much as he thought he should have, and that made him angry with his friends, whom he felt had tricked him in the matter. It also worried him because he had charged the additional expenses to his parents' credit card. He did not have the money to pay the bill and knew he could not get the money from his parents because they had informed him they would no longer cover his excessive spending.

A car horn interrupted Namuh's thoughts. It was his friend Jack with whom he was most upset about the additional expenses. As Jack approached, Namuh felt rage growing in him. He tried to control his intense negative feelings for Jack but could not; he feared what he would have to face with his parents. He was headed down the low road.

Jack smiled and greeted Triune Niarb and asked if he was recovering from the virus. Triune Niarb's response was short and filled with contempt, so Jack asked him what was wrong, and that upset Triune Niarb even more. He appeared to lose control and accused Jack and the others of tricking him into using his parents' credit card to pay all the expenses. This is an example of being on the low road.

Jack appeared surprised about Triune Niarb's accusations and tried to defend the group's actions. Triune Niarb did not accept Jack's explanation. He amplified his claims of unfair treatment by Jack and his friends. It became obvious to Jack that Namuh was not himself and was experiencing an emotional hijacking on the low road. Jack quickly said his goodbyes and left.

Nasty or Angry Triune Niarb (brain) Factors and the Major Brain Regions

An analysis of the Triune Niarb factors will help readers understand why Namuh was angry. First, his survival factors were all very unfavorable. He was facing threats, and all his bodily functions were at their weakest points. He had not received adequate nourishment, rest, or sleep.

Second, his mediating factors were not able to help him stay in touch with himself, and these factors gave him a sense of being out of control in two important areas of his life. The poor state of his health and wealth caused him to be impaired in a third area—his state of wisdom. He was depressed. He thought about the last time he had had such bad thoughts and how it had turned out badly for him.

Jack's visit had evoked Triune Niarb's high-order factors; Jack had arrived in an expensive sports car he had told his friends he would buy after their vacation. That really upset Namuh because his high-order factors made a value judgment—Jack could afford the car because Jack had made Namuh pay all the expenses for the vacation. Niarb began to think about how to pay the credit card bill. His high-order factors told him he would just have to forget his vanity and sell his Rolex, but that increased his resentment of Jack and his new car.

The Normal (human brain) Namuh Niarb

Two weeks passed. Namuh's virus appeared to have run its course, and his sleep and eating patterns were back to normal. He was feeling much better and again eating heart-healthy foods. As he recounted the upsetting event with Jack, Triune Niarb began his trip back on the high road. The issues about the expenses for the trip were much clearer, and he understood what Jack had tried to explain to him. He realized he had overreacted to Jack's request to put the additional charges on his parents' credit card. He remembered Jack telling him he had applied for a car loan and did not want high charges on his credit history before getting the loan. He reminded Namuh that he and his friends had all agreed to pay him back if he would charge their expenses on his parents' credit card.

He had also forgotten that his parents liked to have large charges on their credit cards as long as he paid it back before the end of the month because they would get free points they could exchange for gifts or travel miles. As he traveled back on the high road, he thought of how stupid he must have looked when he had blown up at Jack.

Jack told him that on that previous visit, he had had a check in hand for Namuh, but after seeing how sick and upset Namuh had been, he had left hurriedly without giving him the check. Triune Niarb felt a sense of relief realizing Jack was a true friend and was not angry with him for acting as he did. He was very pleased to know he would not lose the relationship he had with Jack and the others. However, he still had some concerns that his actions might have damaged this relationship.

Triune Niarb apologized to Jack for the way he had reacted; he told Jack that the medicine he had been taking had caused him to lose sleep and his appetite and that was why he had been really out of it when Jack had come by the last time. He explained to Jack what he had been afraid of and why he had feared it. He also admitted to Jack that he had forgotten about the group's promise to pay off the credit card bill. He told Jack his parents were very happy for the extra 10,000 points they got on their credit card statement.

They expressed their amusement over how Triune Niarb had overreacted.

Triune Niarb told Jack that he hoped that would not affect his relationship with the group. He asked Jack to explain the situation to his friends.

Normal or Average Triune Niarb Factors and the Major Brain Regions

After the virus was gone and he was off the medicine, Triune Niarb's bodily functions got back to normal, and he did not feel threatened. He again was eating and sleeping well, and his mediating factors gave him a sense of control over his life. He again saw things as they were and how his previous response had been out of line with reality. Namuh's high-order factors were back; he was able to be in the present with his friends and make personal value judgments about what he had been thinking before Jack arrived. He felt a strong need to explain his action to Jack and ask for his forgiveness.

Jack's high-order factors allowed him to sense Namuh's regret for his out-of-control actions. Jack assured him that their friendship was still strong. They sensed each other's sincere desires to put the unpleasant event in the past, and they began discussing plans for next year's vacation.

Dnim Tirips Luos (*Mind, Spirit, and Soul Spelled Backward*): The Great Wise One from Nevaeh (*Heaven spelled backward*)

Dnim Tirips Luos is Namuh Niarb's human brain's father who is present in Namuh's awareness. You might say that Dnim Tirips Luos is largely responsible for how Namuh develops and behaves. It is often assumed that Niarb (brain) is in control of the Dnim (mind), but I believe Dnim helps control Niarb. Many disagree on where or if Dnim, Tirips (Spirit), and Luos (soul) exist. This disagreement is strongest in much of the scientific community, and it is largely based on the idea that because one cannot give an exact location for Dnim, Trips, or Luos, they must not exist. However, we all agree there is wind, but none of us can specifically identify where it is or see it; we just know the effects it has on the climate. I believe the scientific community should acknowledge the influence of the mind, spirit, and soul on human behavior in much the same way.

One interesting finding from science is on the placebo effect in medicine and the treatment of illnesses and diseases. As previously mentioned, approximately one in every three individuals reports positive results when given a sugar pill or placebo for medical problems rather than drugs or medicine that have known positive effects on the medical problem. Scientists cannot give an accurate explanation for this because they do not know why this happens. I do not mean to deemphasize the value of the sciences but rather to say it takes time and research to uncover what God has created in such an orderly manner. It requires acts of faith to persist in research efforts when there is limited evidence to support such scientific efforts.

Appendix C

How Neuroplasticity Occurs in Our Daily Lives

Imagine being able to change your being by simply changing what you concentrate your thoughts and actions on. Proverbs 23:7 reads, "For as he thinketh in his heart, so is he?" This scripture provides clues as to how the human mind functions with the aid of the brain through neuroplasticity and neurogenesis. Let us return to Namuh Niarb, the eccentric one from India, and examine how neuroplasticity likely occurs.

Namuh Niarb comes to the United States

We find Namuh engaged in his favorite activity—watching CNNN, the cable network I refer to as the Current National Negative News network. Namuh spends at least six hours a day watching this channel. He usually wakes up to the sound of CNNN, and he often falls asleep late at night watching it. He watched CNNN for twelve years in India as a way to learn about American culture, and that greatly influenced his views of Americans. He had formed some negative opinions about different ethnic groups.

However, once in the United States, he had little personal contact with these groups. He worked in Silicon Valley as a computer video game programmer and spent most of his time interacting with people who had educational backgrounds similar to his.

Namuh also liked watching Westerns and action movies because they helped him in his work as a video game programmer. He also had an interest in watching movies and reading books about gang violence in US inner cities. He loved to watch CNNN reports on news stories that repeatedly showed reruns of violent events for hours and sometimes days after the actual violent event had occurred.

Namuh Niarb's Visit to Chicago for the Annual Video Game Conference

One July day in Chicago, Namuh was enjoying the scenes and fun in the Windy City. It happened to be the weekend for one of Chicago's most famous summer events, the Taste of Chicago; thousands were visiting the city in one of its famous parks near the downtown area and Lake Michigan beach; it was a perfect opportunity for Namuh to get an up-close and personal look at what a real American inner-city culture looks, feels, sounds, smells, and tastes like.

Namuh's friends had warned him to be careful about what he did while he was at this event. His friends told him that people might pick his pocket. Nevertheless, Namuh was determined to have this real-life experience because he thought it would help him to be more creative as a video game programmer.

Namuh arrived alone at the park just before dark. He had an uneasy feeling that he could not explain. That feeling intensified as a group of young men approached him. They were very loud while listening to loud soul music. He really became very nervous as he noticed they all wore the same colors. He began to recall things he had read about or seen in movies. He remembered that in movies he had watched, gang members in Chicago wore particular colors so other gang members would recognize them. He had a strong feeling of wanting to get away from these young men. He unconsciously felt for his wallet.

One young man sensed that Namuh was nervous and told him, "Hey man, that's a cool shirt you're wearing! Where are you from?" Namuh nervously responded, "From Silicon Valley." The young man asked, "Where's that?" Namuh replied, "California." The young man said, "Man, you don't look like or sound like you're from California. You sound like you're from India or some other Eastern country." Namuh smiled and said, "You're right. I am from India. How did you guess that?" The young man explained that he had had a six-month study-abroad program in India as part of his college education.

Namuh later learned from the young man that the purple and gold colors the young man and his friends wore were fraternity colors. They were all college graduates and frat brothers as they referred to themselves from all over the United States. The young man explained it was an annual tradition for his fraternity to meet each year at the Taste of Chicago. He introduced his frat brothers to Namuh. They were all very friendly and welcomed Namuh to join them in their celebration.

Namuh could not contain his surprised expressions as he learned about these young men and their professional job titles. Most of them were doctors, lawyers, or business owners. There was one professional basketball player and one well-known political official Namuh had heard about and seen many times on CNNN.

Namuh's Reflections of His Day at the Taste of Chicago

That night back in his hotel room, Namuh began to think about his day in the park. He felt perplexed about his experiences with the young men whom at first he feared but later respected deeply. He tried to figure out why he at first feared these young men and realized he had never been around African American males or had seen movies in which African American males played roles as doctors, lawyers, or business owners. Most movies he had watched featured African American males as the bad people or criminals. He thought about one of the psychology classes he had taken many years ago in which he learned about respondent conditioning made famous by a Russian scientist Ivan Pavlov. He wondered if that was how he had learned to respond to the mere sight of African American males as being a potential group of dangerous individuals.

Analysis of the Normal or Average Triune Brain Parts and How to Explain Implicit Bias, Neuroplasticity, and Neurogenesis

How can one explain why Namuh would fear African American males when he had never really met one? A simple answer would be through the process of respondent conditioning learning, which more than likely led to neuroplasticity that is closely associated with implicit bias. Let us examine more closely how this process works using the above scenario.

Important Points to Consider about the Scenario

First, Namuh had a neutral position toward African Americans prior to his exposure to CNNN and watching violent movies. Second, there was a strong emotional element associated with the exposure to negative news and violent movies that are likely to evoke emotional responses naturally each time Namuh watched the negative news or violent movies. Third, Namuh had daily exposures both consciously and unconsciously. Finally, there was a conscious intent to learn more about the violence in US inner cities. There was a perceived benefit for Namuh to understand and learn about this sector of America's culture in that it would make him a better video game programmer.

Classical Conditioning, Neuroplasticity, and Neurogenesis

Readers familiar with Pavlov's famous experiment that illustrated how classical conditioning works will see the parallel to Namuh's conditioning to respond to African Americans. In Pavlov's experiment, he paired a conditioned stimulus, food, with an unconditioned stimulus, a bell. Each time he would give the experimental dog some food, he would ring a bell. The dog would salivate naturally at the sight of the food at the beginning of the experiment. After many pairing of the food and the bell, Pavlov removed the food and rang the bell. The dog would salivate at the sound of the bell even in the absence of the food.

This same conditioning process is likely what happened with Namuh. Namuh's watching violent movie evoked a strong fear response that made him feel uneasy and fearful (unconditioned response). This fear and uneasy feelings were the natural responses that were elicited by the unconditioned stimuli of violent movies. Prior to Namuh's watching African American males in violent movies paired with the conditioned stimuli of the violent movies, there was a neutral effect on Namuh toward African American males. But after many pairing of African American males and violent movies, this stage was set for an unconditioned response.

Removing the violent movies but being around similar African American males as featured in the violent movies made Namuh feel uneasy and fearful without watching the violent movies. He had had very little if any contact with African American males other than what he saw in the violent movies. The pairing of violent movies and African American males after many exposures became just like what happened in Pavlov's experiment. African Americans males became unconditioned fear-evoking stimuli for Namuh.

Readers might say that Namuh would certainly know the difference between what happened in a movie and what happened in real life. However, it is important to understand that our prior conditioning predetermines much of how we previously responded. Our prior conditioning is often not a conscious or preplanned action on our part. When an unplanned event occurs repeatedly with a strong emotionally latent stimulus, the unplanned event elicits the same strong response as does the emotionally latent stimulus. For example, one only needs to think of the color red and his or her thoughts changes immediately to think of "danger," "unsafe," or "need to be on the alert."

CAUTION: This is the author's attempt at imagining the human brain's functions. This is not a serious attempt to explain neurobiology. Readers should consult the referenced sources for scientific explanations of the human brain functions.

As American citizens, we associate danger with the color red. The color red denotes all stoplights, fire trucks, stop signs, and unsafe places. This is natural and a human learned survival response that exist in our biology, more specifically in our brains, and it supports our decision-making efficiency. In today's media, this is often called implicit bias. If one had lived most of his or her life in another culture where the color red did not denote dangerous situations, his or her responses would be different. We Americans know that the color red does not always mean danger. However, when we see red, our immediate response without any conscious effort on our part is to be cautious or be on the alert for danger.

Just as Pavlov's dog could not prevent the unconscious response of salivation to the sound of the bell even when no food was present, Namuh could not prevent the unconscious response of feeling uneasy and fearful about the African American males he saw in the park. This is true even though he might have rationally known that the African American males posed no threat to him. (Refer to my comments in the sidebar box.)

It is very important to emphasize that implicit bias is part of all humans, but it does mean that when we make quick choices without understanding our tendencies toward implicit bias that it is not acceptable. It is important to have honest and open self-understanding about our unconscious biases.

One of the best ways of knowing how others perceive us is having them give us their open and honest feedback. Once we have such feedback, we must accept it and not deny the respondents' perceptions of us. As mentioned earlier, we all have blind spots about how others perceive us, and we often tend to ignore or dismiss the feedback. It is equally important to know how others perceive us. Once we have this understanding, we are in a much better position to make excellent decisions about managing our emotions.

How Does Classical Conditioning Influence Neuroplasticity and Neurogenesis?

Recent research has revealed that the human brain is able to change relative to its environmental influences by what brain scientists refer to as neurogenesis, and at an even deeper level through epigenetics. A simple way to explain epigenetics is that certain environmental conditions influence gene expression or the turning on or off of certain genes, which could influence neuroplasticity and other brain/mind activities. The interested reader can refer to *Mindsight* by Daniel Siegel and other related references on epigenetics.

Neuroplasticity is the capacity of the brain to change and create new neural connections in response to experience. The brain may be changed at the biological level or in its neuronal structures through three processes. First, one must understand that classical conditioning occurs only with repeated exposure. Second, the number of exposures required for this process to occur depends on the type of stimulus, its emotional latency, and the individual involved. Third, the relationship among neuroplasticity, neurogenesis, and conditioning depends on how focused the individual is on a particular response relating this to what likely happened to Namuh's brain. The three conditions for neuroplasticity to occur were present and likely influenced neurogenesis.

As mentioned, the first condition of repeated exposures was met through Namuh's watching hours of negative emotionally latent news reports on CNNN, violent movies, and videos. Second, Namuh had a long history of repeated exposures to the negative stimuli. He had watched CNNN in India and the United States for years. Finally, he met the condition of focus by his intense concentration on learning about the American culture of violence often portrayed in Westerns and other violent movies that showed African American males as criminals. His focus increased due to his desire to become a better computer gaming programmer.

Appendix D

Sample Emotional Management Assessment Instruments

Exhibit 1: Assessing Thoughts and Feelings (ATF 1 Assessment Instrument)

Part 1

Reflect on your life; think of times when you became very upset with someone. Think of at least five situations and individuals and answer the following about each.

1. What did the person do to cause you to get upset?
2. What were your thoughts about this person? Why do you think he acted as he acted?
3. How did you feel about this person? Why do you think you felt this way?
4. How do you think this person should have acted?
5. How do you know the person felt as you assumed she felt?

Part 2

Analyze your responses by identifying and listing

1. The most reoccurring things that caused you to be upset. Notice what type of person in terms of his or her personality, traits, or

behaviors caused you to be upset. What was most common for all the people who upset you?

2. Your dominant or reoccurring thoughts about the most upsetting individuals.
3. Your dominant or reoccurring feelings about the most upsetting individuals.

Reality Check

After examining your five to seven different situations, determine these.

4. What did you notice about yourself in terms of your expectations about how others should act? What did you learn about yourself?
5. Did you notice any similarities among the individuals in how they felt? Did you notice any similarities in how you reached your conclusions about how the different individuals felt?
6. What have you discovered about yourself as to why you think and feel as you do?

Exhibit 2: Awareness of Relationship Management Skills (ARMS 2 Assessment Instrument)

Part 1: My Perspective

Think about seven to ten individuals with whom you have a personal relationship. These individuals should not involve professional relationships. They could be family members such as spouses, children, in-laws, etc.

Respond to the following questions on one sheet for each individual.

When I am in conversation or interacting in personal relationship with (name) _____, usually,

1. I disagree with what he/she has to say.

Mostly agree	Mostly disagree	Explain

2. I agree with what he/she has to say.

Mostly agree	Mostly disagree	Explain

3. I withhold judgment and just listen to what he/she has to say.

Mostly agree	Mostly disagree	Explain

4. I usually offer my advice even if it is not asked for.

Mostly agree	Mostly disagree	Explain

5. I feel comfortable talking to him/her without a personal agenda.

Mostly agree	Mostly disagree	Explain

6. I feel uncomfortable talking to him/her.

Mostly agree	Mostly disagree	Explain

7. I argue for my point of view when I feel I am right.

Mostly agree	Mostly disagree	Explain

8. I don't argue for my point of view even if I feel I am right.

Mostly agree	Mostly disagree	Explain

9. I show respect for others' opinions even if I feel they are completely out of line with my thinking.

Mostly agree	Mostly disagree	Explain

10. I tell others that their opinions are completely out of line with my thinking.

Mostly agree	Mostly disagree	Explain

Part 2: Others' Perspectives

Think about seven to ten individuals with whom you have a personal rather than a professional relationship. Ideally, this would be the same individuals in part 1 of this exercise. They could be family members such as a spouse, children, in-laws, etc. Ask them to respond to the following questions.

When I am in conversation with (name) _____, he/she usually

1. disagrees with what I have to say, and this makes me feel like _____
2. agrees with what I say, and this makes me feel like _____
3. withholds judgment and just listens to what I have to say, and this makes me feel like _____
4. usually offers advice even if it is not solicited, and this makes me feel like _____
5. makes me feel comfortable in a conversation with him/her because _____
6. does not allow me to share my interests. He or she is usually focused on his or her interests, and that makes me feel like _____
7. argues for his or her point of view when he or she feels that he or she is right, and this makes me feel like _____
8. does not argue for his or her point of view even if he or she feels he or she is right, and this makes me feel like _____
9. shows respect for my opinions even if he or she feels they are completely out of line with his or her thinking, and this makes me feel like _____
10. tells me that my opinions are completely out of line with his or her thinking, and this makes me feel like _____

Other feedback for (name) _____ (optional)

11. I would enjoy our relationship much more if during our conversations you would _____

12. I really appreciate the following things that you do and say when we talk _____

Exhibit 3: Awareness of Professional Relationship Management Skills (APRMS 3 Assessment Instrument)

Part 1: My Professional Relationship Management

Reflect on your professional relationships with your bosses and coworkers. Try to include seven to ten different individuals in your reference group. In your reflections, respond to the following questions:

1. I am effective and respected by my superiors. (Number of superiors ____)
   a. Strongly agree because _____
   b. Agree because _____
   c. Disagree because _____
   d. Strongly disagree because _____

2. I am effective and respected by my coworkers. (Number of coworkers ____)
   a. Strongly agree because _____
   b. Agree because _____
   c. Disagree because _____
   d. Strongly disagree because _____

3. I have an excellent relationship with my superiors. (Number of superiors ____)
   a. Strongly agree because _____
   b. Agree because _____
   c. Disagree because _____
   d. Strongly disagree because _____

4. I feel I am an excellent judge of my professional relationship management skills. (Number of different positions ____)
    a. Strongly agree because _____
    b. Agree because _____
    c. Disagree because _____
    d. Strongly disagree because _____

5. I feel my superiors are excellent at judging my professional relationship skills. (Number of superiors ___)
    a. Strongly agree because _____
    b. Agree because _____
    c. Disagree because _____
    d. Strongly disagree because _____

6. I feel my coworkers are excellent at judging my professional relationship skills. (Number of coworkers ____)
    a. Strongly agree because _____
    b. Agree because _____
    c. Disagree because _____
    d. Strongly disagree because _____

Part 2: Superiors and Coworkers

_____

(Assessed person's title and work relationship)

Think about up to ten individuals with whom you have had a professional relationship in the last three to five years. They should be very familiar with your work experience and should have been co-dependent on your relationship management skills to get their jobs accomplished. The ideal people would be current or previous supervisors or coworkers. Ask them to respond to the following questions.

In my experience in working with (your name) _____,
he/she usually

1. demonstrated professional relationship skills in an
    a. outstanding manner; an example of this was _____
    b. exceptional manner; an example of this was _____
    c. average manner; an example of this was _____
    d. below average; an example of this was _____

2. was accepted and respected by the entire organization; he/she
    interacts with others in an
    a. outstanding manner; an example of this was _____
    b. exceptional manner; an example of this was _____
    c. average manner; an example of this was _____
    d. below average; an example of this was _____

3. was open to feedback from superiors and coworkers in an
    a. outstanding manner; an example of this was _____
    b. exceptional manner; an example of this was _____
    c. average manner; an example of this was _____
    d. below average; an example of this was _____

4. an accurate judge of relationship management skills in his/her role
    as a team player
    a. outstanding manner; an example of this was _____
    b. exceptional manner; an example of this was _____
    c. average manner; an example of this was _____
    d. below average; an example of this was _____

5. demonstrates the importance of having an organizational culture
    that promotes excellent relationship management skills by everyone;
    he/she does this in an
    a. outstanding manner; an example of this was _____
    b. exceptional manner; an example of this was _____
    c. average manner; an example of this was _____
    d. below average; an example of this was _____

Exhibit 4: Awareness of Leadership Effectiveness Skills (ALES 4 Assessment Instrument)

Part 1

The first part of the assessment is for you to complete about yourself. Reflect on how you tend to influence people to accomplish goals for you or your organization. Then, rank each of the three areas listed below using the scale 0 to 10. Use the written descriptions for each of the areas below to assist you in making your rankings. This list comes from *Launching a Leadership Revolution* (Brady and Woodward 2013).

Character(0 to 10)	Tasks(0 to 10)	Relationship(0 to 10)
honesty	acceptance of responsibility	accepting people
integrity	work ethic	approving of people
courage	availability	appreciating people
proper values based on absolute truth	willingness to invest time	seeing the good in people
faith	tenacity	encouraging others
a humble spirit	perseverance	caring for and about people
patience with others	execution	putting others first
discipline	order	seeking win-win arrangements
self-mastery	industry	helping people accomplish tasks
humility	resolution/determination	living the "golden rule"

My Ranking for Character is _____.

My Ranking for Tasks is _____

My Ranking for Relationship is _____

Calculate your leadership effectiveness score by multiplying and summing your score as follows: (example): character score = 5; tasks score = 2; relationship score = 7 (5 x 2 x 7) = 70.

Note: highest possible score is 1,000. Lowest possible score is zero.

Part 2

Find seven to ten people who are very familiar with you and how you tend to lead others. Please ask them to complete this assessment by reflecting on how you tend to influence people to accomplish goals for you or your organization. Then, rank each of the three areas below using the scale 0 to 10. Use the written descriptions for each of the area below to make your rankings.

Character	Tasks	Relationship
honesty	acceptance of responsibility	accepting people
integrity	work ethic	approving of people
courage	availability	appreciating people
proper values based on absolute truth	willingness to invest time	seeing the good in people
faith	tenacity	encouraging others
a humble spirit	perseverance	caring for and about people
patience with others	execution	putting others first
discipline	order	seeking win-win arrangements
self-mastery	industry	helping people accomplish tasks
humility	resolution/determination	living the "golden rule"

My Ranking for Character is _____.

My Ranking for Tasks is _____

My Ranking for Relationship is _____

Calculate your leadership effectiveness score by multiplying and summing your score as follows (example): character score = 5; tasks score = 2; relationship score = 7 (5 x 2 x 7) = 70.

Highest possible score is 1,000. Lowest possible score is zero.

Appendix E

Quotes from the Masters of Emotional Management

Happiness is when what you think, what you say, and what you do are in harmony. —Mahatma Gandhi

You must not lose faith in humanity. Humanity is an ocean; if a few drops of the ocean are dirty, the ocean does not become dirty. —Mahatma Gandhi

To believe in something, and not live it, is dishonest. — Mahatma Gandhi

We must use time wisely and forever realize that the time is always ripe to do right. —Nelson Mandela

There is no passion to be found playing small - in settling for a life that is less than the one you are capable of living. —Nelson Mandela

Resentment is like drinking poison and then hoping it will kill your enemies. —Nelson Mandela

Appendix F

Activity for Fun—Interview Script

Please ask all your subjects to complete this questionnaire below. It does not matter from which group you have initially selected the subjects. Once all subjects complete the questionnaire, their responses will reveal their group. All subjects will have a maximum of ten minutes to respond to these statements.

Happy people are wealthy people. (1)
1. Strongly Agree
2. Agree
3. Agree somewhat
4. Undecided
5. Disagree somewhat
6. Disagree
7. Strongly disagree
People who manage their finances well are usually happy. (2)
1. Strongly Agree
2. Agree
3. Agree somewhat
4. Undecided
5. Disagree somewhat
6. Disagree
7. Strongly disagree

People who believe in the existence of God or a higher power are usually happy and hopeful for a bright future.(3)

1. Strongly Agree
2. Agree
3. Agree somewhat
4. Undecided
5. Disagree somewhat
6. Disagree
7. Strongly disagree

People who identify with the major views of their chosen political leaders are usually happy and well adjusted in their communities.(4)

1. Strongly Agree
2. Agree
3. Agree somewhat
4. Undecided
5. Disagree somewhat
6. Disagree
7. Strongly disagree

People who have definite views on moral values and understand that there are absolute "right" behaviors that one should practice are happy and well adjusted in their communities.(5)

1. Strongly Agree
2. Agree
3. Agree somewhat
4. Undecided
5. Disagree somewhat
6. Disagree
7. Strongly disagree

People who believe that values are relative and it depends on the situation as to whether a particular behavior is moral or immoral are happy and well adjusted in their communities.(6)
1. Strongly Agree
2. Agree
3. Agree somewhat
4. Undecided
5. Disagree somewhat
6. Disagree
7. Strongly disagree

People who believe that the federal government's role in their lives should be limited to national defense issues and that all other issues should be left up to local government and individual control are happy and well adjusted in their communities.(7)
1. Strongly Agree
2. Agree
3. Agree somewhat
4. Undecided
5. Disagree somewhat
6. Disagree
7. Strongly disagree

Individuals who grew up in homes where their parents had strong beliefs in God or a higher power are usually happy and well adjusted in their communities.(8)
1. Strongly Agree
2. Agree
3. Agree somewhat
4. Undecided
5. Disagree somewhat
6. Disagree
7. Strongly disagree

Those whose political views are very conservative are likely to find it difficult to adjust to environments that are mostly liberal. They are likely to be unhappy and adjust poorly in liberal environments.(9)

1. Strongly Agree
2. Agree
3. Agree somewhat
4. Undecided
5. Disagree somewhat
6. Disagree
7. Strongly disagree

Those whose political views are very liberal are likely to find it difficult to adjust to environments that are mostly conservative. They are likely to be unhappy and adjust poorly in conservative environments.(10)

1. Strongly Agree
2. Agree
3. Agree somewhat
4. Undecided
5. Disagree somewhat
6. Disagree
7. Strongly disagree

Those with moderate political views are likely to find it difficult to adjust to environments with conservative or liberal views. They are likely to be unhappy and adjust poorly in either liberal or conservative environments.(11)

1. Strongly Agree
2. Agree
3. Agree somewhat
4. Undecided
5. Disagree somewhat
6. Disagree
7. Strongly disagree

The saying "Money does not make you happy" is outdated today.(12)

1. Strongly Agree
2. Agree
3. Agree somewhat
4. Undecided
5. Disagree somewhat
6. Disagree
7. Strongly disagree

The saying "Money does not make you happy" is too simplistic and ignores the reality of the cost of living and the quality of life that require money.(13)

1. Strongly Agree
2. Agree
3. Agree somewhat
4. Undecided
5. Disagree somewhat
6. Disagree
7. Strongly disagree

I am personally happier when I have enough money to meet my personal and family financial needs.(14)

1. Strongly Agree
2. Agree
3. Agree somewhat
4. Undecided
5. Disagree somewhat
6. Disagree
7. Strongly disagree

I understand that money should be viewed as a tool that can be used for many purposes in my life and it is an important factor to my overall happiness.(15)
1. Strongly Agree
2. Agree
3. Agree somewhat
4. Undecided
5. Disagree somewhat
6. Disagree
7. Strongly disagree

Having an abundance of financial resources is likely to be a major source of unhappiness because of unrealistic expectations from family, friends, associates, and society.(16)
1. Strongly Agree
2. Agree
3. Agree somewhat
4. Undecided
5. Disagree somewhat
6. Disagree
7. Strongly disagree

My faith helps me to have great hope and optimism, which helps me maintain my happiness and positive outlook on life.(17)
1. Strongly Agree
2. Agree
3. Agree somewhat
4. Undecided
5. Disagree somewhat
6. Disagree
7. Strongly disagree

When I feel unhappy, I am usually able to change my thinking and realize how blessed I am in my current state of affairs understanding that my situation could be worse.(18)

1. Strongly Agree
2. Agree
3. Agree somewhat
4. Undecided
5. Disagree somewhat
6. Disagree
7. Strongly disagree

People who say they rely on their faith to help them when they are unhappy are usually superstitious and believe in some form of religion or spirituality without any rational evidence that it works.(19)

1. Strongly Agree
2. Agree
3. Agree somewhat
4. Undecided
5. Disagree somewhat
6. Disagree
7. Strongly disagree

Having hope and optimism is the same as believing in a fortune cookie or a horoscope sign; this does not work and has nothing to do with happiness.(20)

1. Strongly Agree
2. Agree
3. Agree somewhat
4. Undecided
5. Disagree somewhat
6. Disagree
7. Strongly disagree

I am a very happy person. I have formed the habit of being positive and optimistic in all my relationships. I believe that it is very important to practice being positive and optimistic in all situations and relationships.(21)

1. Strongly Agree
2. Agree
3. Agree somewhat
4. Undecided
5. Disagree somewhat
6. Disagree
7. Strongly disagree

Appendix G

Updated References

1 http://www.officer.com/article/12010561/perception-and-insight-in-difficult-times-for-police.

2 http://www.cji.edu/site/assets/files/1921/perceptionandlawenforcement.pdf.

3 http://www.gallup.com/poll/175088/gallup-review-black-white-attitudes-toward-police.aspx.

4 http://bensonhenryinstitute.org/index.php/news-and-events/bhi-news.

5 http://www.casel.org/core-competencies/.

6 C. Lamm and J. Majdandzic, *Neuroscience Research* 90(2015): 15–24.

7 Renée Grinnell, *Internal Locus of Control*. The belief that events in one's life whether good or bad are caused by controllable factors such as one's attitude, preparation, and effort.

8 https://deming.org/management-system/red-bead-experiment.

9 W. Edwards Deming, *Quality, Productivity and Competitive Position*, Massachusetts Institute of Technology, 1982.

10 http://www.naacp.org/criminal-justice-fact-sheet/. A Journey to the Heart of Being Human (Norton Series on Interpersonal Neurobiology) Hardcover, October 18, 2

Acknowledgements

First, I must acknowledge WESTBOW Press and give my sincere appreciation to the entire staff who assisted in the editing, publishing, marketing and distribution process.

Thanks also to the many organizations that have provided professional settings for me to continue to learn and practice my emotional management and organizational systems continuous improvement skills. I will be forever grateful for the institutions that provided the educational opportunities for me to learn the basic knowledge that helped me to later develop the emotional management strategies that I discussed in this book. I am very thankful to have had the privilege and opportunity to complete my undergraduate degree in Industrial Management at Wayne State University, Detroit, Michigan; and Doctorate in Applied Behavioral Analysis with industrial Emphasis at Western Michigan University, Kalamazoo, Michigan.

I would like to acknowledge the four colleges that gave me the opportunity to practice my teaching and mentoring skills on their students and staff. Thanks to the Graduate Colleges that entrusted their students to me to teach and mentor as an Adjunct Professor, Western Michigan University, and Siena Heights University, Michigan. Thanks to Kellogg Community College, Michigan and Jackson College Michigan who employed me full-time as Associate Professor. Also, thanks to the many students that I had the honor of teaching and mentoring during my 30 plus years of teaching. It is very desirable to name some of the most outstanding students that I interacted with, but it's not practical to do so. Any of my former students can locate me at spiritualtyeq.com.

I am thankful for my Psychology Professors at Western Michigan University, Kalamazoo, Michigan who helped me to navigate through the Behavioral Psychology Doctoral process. I am especially grateful for

Doctoral Committee members: Dr Dale Brethower, Dr. Fred Gault, Dr. Neil Kent and Dr. William Redmon. I also thank Dr. Michael Cleary, Professor/Consultant, Wright State University, Ohio for serving on my Doctoral Committee.

I thank the authors of whom I have referenced their research and writings to assist in making the suggested strategies for managing emotions in this book. I thank the LIFE Leadership Learning Organization for giving me the opportunity to learn practical leadership knowledge and to put this knowledge into my daily habit enhancement strategies. I am grateful for having the opportunity to observe since November 2011 this profit oriented organization successfully promote Christian Value/Spirituality.

Finally, I acknowledge my late parents (Eli and Marie Robertson) for being loving and caring parents who taught me to always respect others, to be kind to others; stand up for what's "Right" and to trust God. I am very grateful for my Minster William J. Wyne and the members of Second Missionary Baptist Church for your love and support and giving me the privilege and the honor to serve as your Deacon for the past 10 years. I also thank my siblings (Jerome, Eugene, Melvia, and Barbara), grand children and nephews for your enormous support. A special thank you is extended to my wife Gloria J. Robertson for her love, patience, inspiration and assistance in the writing process of this book. I thank my three children Alysia, Anthony, and Pollis Jr. for their patience, love and support. I must say that you all have made me very proud. Last, but not least, I thank my Heavenly Father for His gifts of Love, Grace, and Mercy that He gives me each day.

Printed in the United States
By Bookmasters